MW00778698

# WRITING THE HEART OF YOUR STORY

## A Guide to Crafting an Unforgettable Novel

C. S. Lakin

Writing the Heart of Your Story: A Guide to Crafting an Unforgettable Novel



Cover designed by Ellie Searl, Publishista®



ISBN-10:0991389441

ISBN-13:978-0-9913894-4-5

Morgan Hill, CA

# Books by C. S. Lakin

## Writing Craft

*Say What? The Fiction Writer's Handy Guide to Grammar, Punctuation, and Word Usage*

## Contemporary Suspense/Mystery

*Someone to Blame*

*Innocent Little Crimes*

*A Thin Film of Lies*

*Intended for Harm*

## Fantasy/Sci-Fi

*The Wolf of Tebron*

*The Map across Time*

*The Land of Darkness*

*The Unraveling of Wentwater*

*The Crystal Scepter*

*The Sands of Ethryn*

*The Hidden Kingdom (2015)*

*Time Sniffers*

## Praise for *Writing the Heart of Your Story*

"A veritable compendium of sound writing advice and technique. Written in a style that is both accessible and fun, Lakin's book will be a welcome companion on your writing journey."

~James Scott Bell, best-selling author of *Conflict and Suspense* and *Plot and Structure*

"C. S. Lakin's addition to the vast oeuvre of 'how to write a novel' wisdom is just that—a fresh and motivating take on conventional wisdom, but with unconventional heart. This is highly accessible teaching that transcends 'how to' and goes deep into 'why to' in a way that will force you to choose between reading it again and jumping on your own project. Bravo."

~Larry Brooks, author of *Story Engineering* and blogger at Storyfix.com

"As authors, our job is to make people feel, and to do this we need to connect with our own deepest selves in the hope we can meet the reader where they are. This book will teach you how to delve into your own heart in order to impact those who read your words."

~Joanna Penn, author of *From Idea to Book* and blogger at TheCreativePenn.com

"I read dozens of writing craft books every year. All too many of them are ho-hum, been-there-done-that. This one is absotively posolutely not. Lakin offers a refreshingly structured—and yet freeing—approach to not just creating a solidly entertaining story, but to crafting a tale of emotional resonance and resilience. Her useful writing exercises and spot-on story sense offer epiphany after epiphany. This is one I will read and reread."

~K. M. Weiland, author of *Outlining Your Novel* and *Structuring Your Novel*

"C. S. Lakin once again shares her generous heart and knowledge and experience with writers in this inspiring and inspired Writing the Heart of Your Story. Ready to take your writing to the next level? Lakin offers practical exercises and clear examples to help you bring heart to your own stories."

~Martha Alderson, author of *The Plot Whisperer* series of writing books

"In Writing the Heart of Your Story, C. S. Lakin won't just lead you through the basic process of writing a novel, from plotting to writing your first paragraph, from finishing your rough draft to editing, she will challenge you at every step to do the hard work of finding the throbbing heart hidden somewhere at the center of your story. This is bloody work and not for the faint of heart. However, Lakin has a confident and experienced kindness that will leave you encouraged to take on even the most sanguine story."

~Joe Bunting, author of *Let's Write a Short Story* and blogger at TheWritePractice.com

"C.S. Lakin provides solid, thoughtful advice to writers with her resource Writing the Heart of Your Story. Susanne's book is filled with practical tips and inspiration to guide and support writers of all experience levels."

~Elizabeth Craig, mystery author and blogger at MysteryWritingIsMurder.blogspot.com

"As a blogger, nonfiction author, and book coach with one novel I'd love to 'fix,' I found Writing the Heart of Your Story just the guide I needed for all the work I do. No boring, tedious lessons here. Instead a fiction craft book full of heart that I could take to heart and put to use. I'll be recommending it to my fiction clients as well!"

~Nina Amir, author of *How to Blog a Book* and blogger at WriteNonFictionNow.com

# Table of Contents

# Part One: It's All about the Heart

## Chapter 1: Targeting the Heart

*"The way is not in the sky. The way is in the heart."*

~Buddha

What would you say is the difference between a good book and a great one? Between a forgettable novel and a classic that lingers long in your memory, maybe even for years? Between a book with a title and plot you've forgotten mere days after you read it and one with lines that haunt you for years, and characters that seem so real you find yourself thinking about them over a lifetime and wondering what they would say or do in a given situation? Some good books provide an entertaining read, much like a good meal will satisfy. But then there are *those other* books.

You know the ones I mean. Those are the ones you hope you'll find as you look for something significant to read, the ones you earnestly search for as if seeking a precious gem, with the desperate hopefulness of a miner panning for gold, day in and out, waiting for the big strike. For when we find that rare book, we drink it in, the way a wanderer long lost in the desert falls upon an oasis full of cool, refreshing life-giving water. A book with that kind of magic—that resonates with our heart and somehow fulfils a need in our soul—that is the mother lode. Books like that are more than just a good, or even great, read. They speak to us on some integral, deep level and nourish us. They speak to our heart.

If your greatest desire as a novelist is to reach and affect a reader's heart in a significant way, to "strike home" with some theme, message, or emotional resonance, then the lessons and observations in this book can be your guide. Drawn not only from my own decades of writing, editing, and reading great (and lousy) books but also from gems of wisdom from a great variety of writing instructors, *Writing the Heart of Your Story* is an amalgam created for one specific purpose—to show writers how to aim, shoot, and hit the bull's eye when it comes to targeting a reader's heart.

## How to Target the Heart

So, as a writer, how do you do that—target the heart of a story? Is there some secret, or a trick to it? Do those "great" writers who write timeless, unforgettable books use some arcane method or formula that no one knows about? Nope. But I would venture to say they have a drive or need to do more than put a bunch of interesting words on a page—or appeal to the masses in order to sell a certain number of copies. They not only have a story to tell, they want to tell it passionately. They have a story with heart, that will appeal to the heart, and they delve into their own hearts to tell it.

Ah . . . there's the key—being brave, daring, and vulnerable enough to get into the deep, scary feelings that are stored in the heart. For, if writers do not go deep, their writing won't either. If their writing doesn't drag them long into late-night hours with grabbing intensity, it won't keep anyone else up reading either. If their writing doesn't possess them and draw life from them in order to come alive, the story will be flat, and maybe even feel dead. Lifeless. Boring.

So, to breathe life into a story, you have to get its heart pumping. It's been said that the heart is the seat of motivation. Jesus is quoted in the Bible as saying, "Out of the heart's abundance the mouth will speak." If the heart of our story is abundant with rich themes and motifs and passion, the "mouth" [read: author via ten typing fingers] will express them. But you first have to know *how* to get to the heart of your story. Sometimes you have to mine deep into the caverns of your heart before you find what you are looking for. And it may take some time. Each story you mine will be different, and will require a new journey on perhaps unmapped trails and dimly lit tunnels. But this book will show you how to do this, regardless of what genre you are writing in, one simple step at a time.

## Nothing New under the Sun

Some of what is contained in this book may not at all be new to you. I'm not claiming I have some brand-new method that will rock your world. I can only bring to my students and editing clients whom I mentor what I have learned over the twenty-five years I've been writing novels (and the fifty-plus years I've been voraciously reading them). There are hundreds of writing craft books "out there" and thousands of instructive blog posts and magazine articles that will teach you technique on every aspect of novel writing. But I've yet to see one book that centers on this very necessary topic on how to get to the heart of a story.

Be aware that this is not solely about technique or craft or method. Those things are included to some degree and are important, but they are mostly tools for you to carry and use along the way as you excavate through the walls of rock to reach the heart of your story.

## The Road That Few Writers Take

Think of this excursion as a holistic endeavor—a joining of mind and heart. For many writers, constructing a novel is mostly a "mind" exercise. Some check their emotions, personal feelings, and experiences at their office door and dive into writing with full-throttle brain power. Even so doing, a person can learn to write well enough [read: technique, craft] to evoke particular emotions and reactions in a reader, and thus be successful in producing a very strong novel that may get acclaim. But as G. K. Chesterton so aptly noted: "There is a road from the eye to the heart that does not go through the intellect."

That's the less-traveled road we want to explore. That road takes you to a deeper level than you can reach with your intellect, and if you've ever had a moment when you've written a mind-blowing sentence or paragraph, or you've found tears streaming down your face as you reread a passage you just wrote (okay, maybe you too are thinking about that scene in *Romancing the Stone*, in which romance writer Joan Wilder is reading the end of her novel and weeping away), you know there is that special place a writer can get to, a Shangri-la or nirvana where magic happens. Where you reach the heart, and it's pumping wild and strong.

For some of us writers, that's the place we aim to get to every time we sit down to write. That's the runner's high, or the climber's euphoria. No, we aren't striving to get there to grab a temporary thrill that will fade after a few hours. We strive to get to that place because it's the most genuine, most truthful, barest center of our existence.

If that sounds a little too corny to you, then maybe this book isn't really for you. And that's okay. But some of us have caught a glimpse of this kind of heaven, and we want to live there. Or at least know how to navigate to it so we *can* get there if we put our minds (and hearts) to the task.

So, are you ready? Grab your picks and shovels, and follow me.

Think About . . . some of your favorite novels. Grab a few off the shelf and read just the first scene. Highlight some lines that stand out to you, that seem powerful, original, gripping. Start a notebook in which you write down a few great lines from various novels' opening scenes, and make a comment about the way the book hooked you and kept you reading. Now, set these books aside to return to later as we go through the important components of opening scenes, and you'll be sure to see things you never noticed before.

## Chapter 2: The Entrance to the Mother Lode

*"What is uttered from the heart alone will win the hearts of others to your own."*
~Goethe

The heart of your story is not located in one spot, like the heart in your body. It's more like a vein of gold threading through the mountain of plot, character, and dialog. At times it might appear a thin strand and at other times a giant pocket of richness, but it is present from the first line of your novel to the last.

Think about the expression "striking a vein." I imagine a miner—sweaty, exhausted, maybe even close to despairing—swinging his pickaxe one last time before heading back to his makeshift camp along the Trinity River in the northern Sierras of California. As metal chomps at the crumbling hillside and rocks and debris fly into the air, a sparkling strip of gold is revealed. What a stroke of luck!

Fortunately, we don't have to swing aimlessly on a hunch. We can determine just where that vein is we're hoping to strike, and then we can use care to aim and direct each swing of the axe so that we're right on target. I would be remiss not to make mention here of a more literal reference of "striking a vein," for when attempting to reach the heart of our story, we also want to cut open a vein and let the blood flow. Forgive me if this sounds a bit morbid, but sometimes in attempting to write a passionate, powerful story, it feels like we're opening a vein and pouring out our lifeblood. Not that writing should be painful; I personally feel it shouldn't have to be—unless someone is forcing us to do it against our will. (I think Stephen King wrote a novel about that!)

Part of that "pain" many writers face when crafting a novel is due to a lack of deep exploring and mapping first. If you are going to excavate a site to find a vein you know is somewhere inside the heart of a mountain you are journeying to, you need to do your homework. If you haven't pored over the geological surveys and journals of those who have gone before you, you also may end up swinging your pickaxe mindlessly, hoping for a strike, but spending months—maybe even years—of your life futilely striving and hoping you'll hit that vein, and getting just as discouraged and despairing as that miner I mentioned.

## Supporting the Tunnel to Avoid Collapse

Digging to the heart takes advance preparation, and I'm not referring to spending time plotting out your story (which is essential). I'm talking about setting up the infrastructure and pathways to get you there.

Think of the old classic movie *The Great Escape*—do you remember it, starring Steve McQueen and James Garner? Based on a true story that took place in 1942, the Germans built what they considered was an escape-proof POW camp, where they planned to house all the problem POWs—i.e., those that had made multiple escape attempts in the past. What the Germans don't realize is that they'd put all the best escape minds in one location.

Undaunted, the prisoners plan one of the most ambitious escape attempts of World War II. They dig three massive tunnels to span across the camp and out under the fences (although when they pop up from underground, they realize they're twenty feet short of freedom). In order to create these long tunnels that don't collapse, they not only have to clear away all the dirt without the task being noticed, they also have to build supports so that the tunnels don't cave in.

Just look at photos and films of commercial mining operations and you'll see the same thing—strong support structures are installed first before any serious mining begins. Only a fool would start digging underground without taking care against collapse.

So too, a writer needs to do the advanced structural work so that her story doesn't "collapse" upon entering. And a great many do collapse—sometimes by the second chapter. So, would it surprise you to learn that the bulk of the work—setting up the framework to support your entire novel—has to mostly take place in the first scene or two? Just as the entrance into the tunnel sets the pattern for the entire supportive structure leading to the mother lode or to "freedom," most of what you will learn in this book pertains directly to your first chapter.

## The First Chapter Carries a Great Burden

Really? When this content was presented in 2012 on my blog Live Write Thrive as a year-long instructional course, the first five months were spent on the first scene. Does that sound a little front-end heavy? Yep. But there's a very good reason. In order to get to the heart of your story, the path must be set up clearly in the first pages of your novel. Most authors know that the beginning or opening of a novel is the most crucial and carries the weightiest burden of any other scene or chapter in your entire book. The opening scene must convey so many things that often the author will have to rewrite it numerous times to get it right, and sometimes the best time to rewrite the opening scene is when your novel is done. Why? Because at that point you have (hopefully) developed your rich themes and motifs, thoroughly explored your protagonist's heart and character arc, and have brought your plot to a stunning and satisfying conclusion.

## Your Opening Scenes Support the Entire Novel

As the first one or two scenes carry the burden of the whole book, they are the "entrance to the mine." If they don't have the correct structure to hold back the tons of dirt [read: the next 70,000 words or more] overhead from falling, you're looking at a potential (or probable) collapse of the whole story. No way will the miners make it to the heart, where the big pocket of gold awaits. More than likely they will be choking on dust and crawling and clawing their way back out to a place they can lick their wounds, clean up a bit, and then ponder how in the world they will find another way in. Whereas, they could have successfully journeyed to the heart had they but taken the time to reinforce the opening.

Which is exactly what this book will be centering on more than anything else—reinforcing the opening of your story in the first scenes so that the reader can safely and excitedly journey through the twists and tunnels of an unforgettable adventure and end up right where you want them to be. By forging a path straight to the heart of your story, you will get right to the heart of your reader. If your heart leads correctly, the reader's heart will follow. It may sound simple, and in a sense it is. Confucius said it succinctly: "Wherever you go, go with all your heart."

## Starting Is Better Than Finishing

There's an ancient proverb that goes like this: "Finishing is better than starting." And therein lies great wisdom, to be sure. I can start a whole lot of projects, but the real test of perseverance, success, and merit is in the finishing. However . . . when it comes to writing a great novel, starting is more important than finishing—at least when it comes to the importance of your major story elements. If you have every essential thing in place in your first scene, you will have set up the entire book in a way that will lead you wonderfully to the finish line.

## The Heart Is the Big Picture

Too many writers just jump in and throw together a first scene for their novel without taking the time to look at *the heart of the story* or *the big picture.* There are plenty of instructional books, websites, and blogs with great content covering every major element and technique needed to write a great novel, but few if any are really focusing on the big picture and the heart of what makes your novel terrific.

Many literary agents and acquisition editors complain that despite good writing overall, many books are missing something. They don't inspire, move, or touch the heart—and yes, believe it or not, those folks *do* expect to have that experience, at least in part, upon reading your first opening scene.

Impossible? Not at all. I have read some unbelievably powerful, moving, heart-wrenching first scenes—and those books were most often big best sellers. That's not to say all best sellers succeed at stirring this type of reaction—far from it! But those gems of books that can so move the reader so quickly are noticed. Big-time. And I believe that's because the author has taken the time to step back and look at the big picture—what lies at the heart of her story.

## The First-Page Checklist

I am often asked to do one-on-one critiques at writers' workshops and events, and because those appointments are usually a scant fifteen minutes long, I came up with a way to dive into each writer's story in that short time. They are instructed to bring page one of their novel, and in that short span of time I read it, then go over a number of important elements that need to be on the first page—using my handy "First-Page Checklist."

Granted, not everything on the list *must* be on page one, but the idea is to be aware of all the elements needed to appear early in a novel—in order to set up that strong entrance to the mine. I believe that the closer to page one you can get all these components, the better. I have heard other writing instructors say similar things in their workshops as well. Without sending you into cardiac arrest by listing nearly twenty important items you need in that first scene, I'm going to concentrate on some important ones—the ones that really need to be considered.

So here, and also available for download from my website using this link, is the First-Page Checklist. (If you are reading the print version of this book, you can type this URL into your browser: http://www.livewritethrive.com/wp-content/uploads/2012/01/first-page-checklist.pdf)

## First Page Checklist

___ Opening Hook: Clever writing and image that grabs the reader
___ Introduction of main character in first few lines
___ Starting the story in the middle of something that's happened (or happening)
___ A nod to setting; avoid excessive exposition or narrative
___ A catalyst, inciting incident, or complication introduced for your character
___ A hint at character's immediate intentions
___ A hint at character's hidden need, desire, goal, dream, fear
___ Unique voice/writing style
___ Setting the tone for the entire book
___ A glimpse at character's personal history, personality—shed light on motivation
___ Introduction of plot goal
___ A course of action/decision implied: introduction of high stakes/dramatic tension
___ Pacing: jump right into present action. No backstory

Think of:

- One characteristic to reveal that makes your character heroic and vulnerable
- One element of mystery, something hinted at that raises curiosity
- One element out of the ordinary, unusual, that makes your book different/stand out
- Concise, catchy dialog (if in the first scene) that is not boring or predictable
- A way to hint at your theme, if you have one

We'll be going over these elements in the various chapters in this book, but here's a simple list to whet your whistle:

- Introduction of the plot goal for the book
- Determining the Major Dramatic Query (MDQ) for your main character
- Opening hook
- Hint of protagonist's visible goal, intentions, need
- Delving into an inciting incident or moment of conflict
- Sympathetic introduction of your protagonist
- A nod to setting
- Establishing tone and voice

So be prepared to begin *at the beginning* to mine your way to the heart of your story. If you start well, I am confident you will finish well. A well-built foundation ensures a solid house, but, well, you may have heard what Jesus said in his Sermon on the Mount about the man who built his house on sand. When the wind and waves [read: the critics and reviewers of your novel] lashed at the house, it crumbled. Jesus referred to that kind of person as being foolish. The fact that you are reading this book tells me you don't want to be cast in with that guy who was left scratching his head at the ruins of his house, wondering what he did wrong. And just as with any building structure, it's all about the foundations—the materials and design used to ensure that house or skyscraper or whatever you have delineated on those blueprints before you will stand the test of time. You can "build" you novel so it, too, stands the scrutiny of critics and has lasting power as it speaks to untold people regardless of time or place.

### My Caveat

Of course, there are always exceptions to every rule, and I'm sticking my caveat in here right now. This is my method and what I have determined is the best "way" into the tunnel to get to the heart of your story. You are welcome to disagree with some or most of what I present, but, for the fun of it, come along with me as I lead you through these tunnels and see what you pick up. If it's only a small chunk of gold here and there, who's to say the trek was a wasted effort? I hope, though, that you will load up your sack with gold, and you'll get so proficient in establishing a firm structure for your mining operation that it will serve you time and again with each novel you write—leading the reader to the heart of your story.

Think about . . . the novel you are presently working on—whether you've finished a draft or are just in the plotting stage. Take some time to think about the first scene you have in mind and whether it holds the potential to reveal all the necessary components needed in a first scene. Grab one or two of those favorite novels you looked at earlier and highlight the items in the First-Page Checklist as you encounter them in each novel's first scene. This will help you start to see how other authors build that entry to their story's mine.

## Chapter 3: Unloading the Nonessentials

*"Words, words, mere words, no matter from the heart."*
~William Shakespeare

Before we begin to shore up the mine shaft leading to the heart of our story, we should examine which materials we need and those we should ditch. No sense hauling a huge load of useless, even detrimental, materials up that long, winding road if they aren't going to help us accomplish our goal. There is nothing worse than expending valuable time and energy on building something that you will just have to throw out, right?

I am truly astonished at how many successful authors (some who put out a best seller each year) spend months writing draft after draft of their novel, tossing each draft in the trash before they finally get the story fixed in their mind well enough to write the "keeper." No wonder these authors tell me how stressful writing is to them, how they often hate their vocation and struggle with every word on every page. I can't help but wonder why they've chosen the method they have and stick with such a painful, wasteful process when they could have a much more enjoyable time creating.

I picture them hauling a heavy iron cart full of weighty building materials up a steep hill, week after week. Then, upon arriving at the top of the mountain where sits the entrance to their mine, they sift through their cart, tossing one giant item after another over their shoulder in realization they really can't use it, until all that's left in the "useful" pile is a handful of nails or a few short two-by-fours. With great weariness they realize they have to make yet another trip down the hill to get more supplies, but rather than make a list, they stumble on, unsure of what they need, without a plan or blueprint, and repeat this same futile process over and over again.

## "I Just Can't . . ."

Sounds harsh? I suppose it is. Some writers say they cannot write at all if they plot anything out. They can't seem to find their creativity or come up with a story if they try to work any of the details out in advance. Some throw up their hands and say, "I can't plot. I'm a 'seat-of-the-pants' writer. I need to let my creativity flow, let the muse take me, wait for inspiration . . ." I understand that mind-set—I truly do. But if you are one of those people, I want to say this to you: I don't believe this is your only choice. I don't believe that if you took the time to set up all the needed elements in advance to provide a sturdy, clear entrance to your mine that you would *not* be able to write your story. I *do* believe it's a matter of determination and choice.

We are not victims of our nature and personality. Would a surgeon say, "I just don't feel I can stitch up this patient's injury that fast and in the recommended way? I need to go at my own speed and be spontaneous so as not to compromise my style or talent or gift. If the patient dies, oh well. I need to be true to who I am"?

Granted, writing a novel is not a life-or-death matter (although sometimes we feel it is). But it is something that requires a skill set and proficiency of craft. Some artists choose to paint spontaneously without much advance thought—just let the brush strokes come and the colors fly. Some artists create masterpieces that way. The same goes for dancers and street poets and musicians. There can be great art produced without planning or preparation—bits of genius expressed that pour from the heart and soul, and spontaneity can be a beautiful thing.

But I will venture to say writing a full-length novel is a bit different from creating a poem off the top of your head. A novel comprises thousands and thousands of words. Each word must somehow string together with other words into sentences and paragraphs and scenes and chapters and create a holistic, cohesive whole. Throwing one hundred thousand words into a blender and spilling them out onto a page does not a brilliant novel make. There are way too many elements that must fit together beautifully, and every word should count and every nonessential piece discarded.

With that said, let's take a look at the most important element that needs to be omitted from your first chapters—backstory.

## Take a Backseat, Backstory!

Okay, we've heard that forever. But it's true. In order to start your story with a punch and draw your reader in, you need to construct a scene happening right here and now (or with something in the past, like a historical, right then and now). Regardless of the semantics here, you get the point.

Some writing instructors say things like "no backstory in the first fifty pages." Some editors at publishing houses will be so bold as to say they would be happy if they saw *none* in an entire book. Maybe that won't quite work for your book, but it's sad to say that countless scenes start with a line or two in the present, and then, *whoosh*! There you are reading about the character's early life or marriage or something she did right before the scene started. Which should make you ask . . .

Are you really starting your story in the right place? More often than not, the answer is no. That's what second and third drafts are for—throwing out your first scene or two.

At the Breakout Novel workshop given by Donald Maass that I attended, he commented that a good number of novel submissions he reads should really be starting with chapter three or four. He noted that a lot of beginning writers spend ten, twenty, or thirty pages just "setting up" the story by explaining a mountain of information they think the reader must have before the story can actually be underway.

In an exercise he had us do, we went through the first thirty pages of our novel, removed every single instance where we used backstory or informative narration, and then chose only three brief sentences containing a "backstory fact" we felt we *really* must include in the opening chapters so the reader would "get" the story. These three sentences were to be conveyed by the protagonist in dialog to another character (forcing us to avoid narrative and share backstory via dialog, which is usually the best way to do so) or as a thought in the character's head. Needless to say, when asked, we students all agreed our novels read much better without the backstory, and we had indeed learned our lesson.

## Give Readers Some Credit

So think about weaning yourself off the need to explain—or as it's put in writer's circles, RUE: Resist the Urge to Explain. Your readers aren't dumb—really! They don't need you to explain everything, and they actually enjoy a mystery and being allowed to start figuring out the puzzle you are presenting. Don't just eliminate backstory—think about all that excessive explanation and narrative and description that goes on and on and delays the reader getting into the mine shaft to take the journey you want them to take.

## Dump the Excessive Explanation

Every time an author stops the present action of a scene to explain, it's akin to a playwright stepping on stage in the middle of an act, pushing aside the actors, and telling the audience something she thinks they absolutely have to know about why or how she wrote the play or what is really going on behind the scenes. I wouldn't be surprised if the audience started throwing tomatoes at the writer and yelling, "Get off the stage! We didn't come to see *you*!"

That's exactly what the reader feels like when the author of a novel interrupts a scene to give "a word from your sponsor." No one likes commercials, right? When the commercial comes on, we get up and go into the kitchen to find something to eat. When a reader encounters a bunch of backstory and tedious explanation, they skim over it until they get back to the "real" story.

Most of the books I read and edit don't "get going" until page twenty or thirty. All that up-front explaining, narrative, setting up the scene, etc., was all great back in Dickens's time (*A Tale of Two Cities*, for example), but we don't do that anymore. TV, movies, and video games have changed the modern reader's tastes. Readers today want cinematic writing. Sol Stein in his book *Stein on Writing* says, "Twentieth-century readers, transformed by film and TV, are used to seeing stories. The reading experience for a twentieth-century reader is increasingly visual. The story is happening in front of his eyes." This is, of course, even more true in the twenty-first century.

## A Better Way

So how do you avoid the dreaded info dump and backstory? Think about the emotion, feeling, or sensation you want to evoke in your reader. You want to put them in a mood right away. You want to be specific to generate that mood, which means bringing in all the senses and showing your character in the middle of a situation, right off the bat.

And that's the next essential element: establishing immediately (did I say immediately?) the drives, desires, needs, fears, frustrations of your protagonist. Not only do you need to show her in conflict, in the midst of a situation that showcases all those things, you also need to reveal her heart, hint at her spiritual need, show her vulnerability, and what obstacles are standing in her way. In the first scene? Oh yes. Yes. We'll look at all of this. And in later chapters I'll clue you in on the three most crucial things you must know about your character and must hint at in the first scene.

Think about . . . going through your first scene and taking out all the backstory. If needed, come up with only one or two lines that tell a little important information you think the reader must know and use those in dialog, if possible. Then read your scene over and see how much better it is. Pull out some of your favorite novels and with a yellow highlighter mark all the backstory in the first scene. If there is any, note how much and in what way it is presented. Learn something neat? Write it down in your notebook.

## Chapter 4: Plot Goals—Seeing Is Believing

*"A goal is a dream with a deadline."*
~author Napoleon Hill

The most essential of essentials in your first scene is setting up your visible plot goal. Did I say visible? Yep. Why? Because if you ask writers what their protagonist's plot goal is, you will often get answers like "she finds love in the end" or "he finally sees his dream realized." Those kinds of answers are not easy to visualize. They're not specific. If I were to write that in a movie script, it would make no sense. Think about how this scene would look on the big screen.

What does "she finds love in the end" translate to visually? Do you see your heroine getting on a plane after quitting her high-glamour New York City job and flying to the jungles of Central America, where her swarthy, ecstatic fiancé is pacing on the torn-up runway awaiting her arrival as a downpour of rain pelts him? You can picture this, right? And so, as you think about your entire book, the ending of the story (which you may not have thought about yet), and most importantly the opening scene, you need to be able to formulate a visible picture of a visible goal. Granted, the details may change. Your heroine may end up getting off the plane in Paris instead of Guatemala City, but you need a visible goal for your protagonist to work toward, and it must be hinted at in the first scene, preferably the first page or two.

## Why Should I Keep Reading?

Sounds crazy? Well, I speak truth! I have been to numerous writing workshops taught by the big-name writing teachers, and they are in agreement (and I know that doesn't mean they are totally right). You can ignore this if you want, but I'm hoping you won't (because I think you'll be sorry). Why is this so important? Because too many novels start off and go on for chapters without the reader having a clue as to what the book is about, what the protagonist is doing or what he/she actually wants, or what the protagonist's goal for the book is. Without any of that, the reader is going to ask "Why should I keep reading?" And rightly so.

When I pick up a novel, if I can't figure out what the heck the protagonist is up to by the end of the first scene (barring the exception of a prologue that doesn't feature said protagonist), I start getting antsy. I might push myself through the next chapter ever hopeful, but if I still don't "get" what the book is about, see some visible goal, care for the poor protagonist who has obstacles the size of the Empire State Building in her way to reach her visible goal, then I usually give up. I can't tell you how many "great" novels I have started (often recommended by friends) that I have done this with.

I admit I'm a tough critic (you can guess why), but if I find even a few redeeming things in the first chapter, I will give a weak-starting book the benefit of the doubt. But not for long. You've got to really reel me in with something—beautiful language, intriguing premise or world, or a hooking mystery—for me to set aside my need to know what the protagonist's visible goal is. And I don't think I'm really the exception to the rule. Most readers want to know this too.

Let me mention something that I'll cover shortly, just in case the "goal" issue seems daunting. The actual goal your protagonist goes after won't be firmly in place until about one-fourth through the novel. In fact, most well-structured novels and screenplays, don't introduce a goal at all until that mark. So I am not saying that from scene one the character must know *exactly* what they want or where they are going—which is the end point of the book. It's the character's *outer motivation* that must be established right away. By revealing his passion, core need, heart's desire from the opening scene, we get a *hint* at that goal, what he will go after when the right set of circumstances pushes him through that "door of no return." A hint is all you need, but it's needed.

## Five Basic Goals—That's All, Folks

In a workshop I took with screenwriter/consultant Michael Hague, I noted the point he made that there are really only five general visible goals characters go after (and he's speaking about movies—his arena—but this does apply to novels as well). Here they are:

- The need to win—competition, the love of another, etc.
- The need to stop—someone, something bad from happening, etc.
- The need to escape
- The need to deliver—a message, one's self, an item, get to a destination (think Cold Mountain with Inman's need to get home. I picture Nicole Kidman speaking in the movie trailer: "Come back. Come back to Cold Mountain." A perfect example of a visible goal set at the start and followed through to the end.)
- The need to retrieve (think Indiana Jones and just about every action-adventure movie. There's always a magic ring, a hidden or lost treasure, or a lost love.)

## Make It Visible or We Can't See It

If you write spiritual character-driven novels like I do, it may be hard to figure out the visible goal. I always seem to start with the spiritual and emotional goals like "she finds peace inside knowing she can't change certain things." Okay, well that's a start. And I know as I plot my novels it's only a start—because I have to then translate that into plot. Visible plot.

In my relational drama/mystery *Someone to Blame* I wanted the reader, at the end, to care for the antisocial, bad-guy antagonist Billy Thurber. I wanted "the reader to care for him in the end." Well, that was vague. But I worked out a visible goal (that he actually didn't know was to occur, but I did), and when he literally uncovers what he has been searching for (or running from), he arrives at the spiritual and emotional place I wanted him to be in. But I had to come up with a visible goal for him.

But wait—he's not my protagonist. Does that mean . . . ? I hope you have come to the conclusion I'm setting up here, because, yes, not just your protagonist but all your major players have to have a visible goal. If your hero's goal is to retrieve the lost Ark of the Covenant, then your antagonist's visible goal is to stop the hero from reaching that goal.

Setting up a plot goal sounds simple, and really, it is. If you have no clue what the plot goal is for your character, then maybe you don't really have a novel ready to be written.

I'm surprised at how many novels I critique for clients that have no plot goal whatsoever. Throughout the critique I find myself writing comments like "What does your character want? What is her goal? What does she need to do or have happen? Why is she doing this . . . ?"

Oftentimes writers really don't know what their book is about, or they have a nebulous plot idea that sounds generally intriguing, but when pressed to say what the character's goal is for the book, they can't come up with anything. Some may disagree, but a plot without a protagonist with a need (or goal) really is no plot at all. Someone in your book has to want something, right? Well, what is that something?

## Visible Plot Goal Gets a Twist

Now, just when you thought you figured this plot goal stuff out, I want you to think about putting a twist or kink in the goal. This is a very common, standard plot device in many novels and in many great movies you see, and it involves a shift in the protagonist's plot goal near the start of the story. This may seem confusing, but let me explain.

You want to show your protagonist in her ordinary world in some way at the start (but don't keep her there too long). Dorothy, in *The Wizard of Oz*, hates living in Kansas, where life is the pits. Even the film is gray and dingy, making the viewer really commiserate with her when she sings "Somewhere over the Rainbow." What's Dorothy's immediate visible goal? Why, to run away to someplace better, someplace safe for her and Toto. But what happens?

Not too long after the story begins, *an incident occurs* that shifts Dorothy from her original goal and sets her on another path toward a different goal—the goal that's *much more important* to her emotionally and spiritually. The tornado whisks her to Munchkinland, and suddenly Dorothy develops a dire need to get home (the place she was initially trying to run away from).

Ah, this is the *real* visible goal of the story, but it got thrust upon the heroine on her way somewhere else. Like Bugs Bunny always said, "I must have taken a left turn at Albuquerque." Yes, your hero will get waylaid early on and be forced to take a new direction, and that will introduce the visible plot goal to be reached by the end of the story—the *real* plot goal of the story.

### The Real Visible Goal

Think about Shrek. All he wants at the start of the story is to get rid of the annoying fairy-tale creatures who are invading his swamp. So he journeys to the center of the kingdom to complain to Lord Farquaad (who came up with that spelling?). But something happens that throws Shrek in a new direction. Sure, the ruler will grant his wish—*but only* if he goes to rescue Princess Fiona and bring her back. And thus begins Shrek's journey to his visible goal—which also involves his true inner journey to find his true self.

Think about Maria in *The Sound of Music*. Her initial goal at the convent is to figure out where she fits in and to leave the convent and get a job. She can't cut it as a nun, and the nuns consider her a problem (I'm humming "How Do You Solve a Problem like Maria?"). But something happens when she becomes a nanny to all those crazy kids. Her visible goal then shifts to want to become a mother to them and find love by marrying the brooding dad, although she thinks her goal is impossible.

No doubt you can come up with a dozen movies and novels in which the hero or heroine starts off wanting one thing but then gets pushed through a door where his visible goal changes. You don't have to write every novel like this, but I wanted to give you some things to consider. There is nothing wrong with introducing your protagonist in the first scene with a visible goal that will stick until the end.

Frodo is happy sitting around at Bag End in Hobbiton until Gandalf sends him off to Rivendell with the ring. Yet, you could argue that when he gets to Elrond's lovely home, his plot goal gets a twist when he realizes he is the best person (hobbit?) to take on the task of destroying the ring. That plot twist happens quite late in the book—in fact, at the end of book one, but all the same, Frodo's plot goal does get a twist that veers him off in the direction needed for him to also reach his spiritual and emotional goals for the story. Your inciting (triggering) incident in the first scene can send your protagonist on her way toward one set goal. But you can also present the goal this way, with a turn at Albuquerque. Both work.

## All Roads Lead to Rome (or Home?)

See, the reason for establishing this visible goal right at the start is it acts as a focusing lens. All roads (scenes) lead to Rome (the goal). So as you write your novel, you will keep this goal in view, and set every obstacle you can to prevent your hero from reaching that goal. It sounds formulaic and simple, but most great novels and films will basically have these elements ingrained in them. Why? Because they are intrinsic to storytelling, and they resonate within us as true story patterns.

Of course, you can do what you want and veer off the tried-and-proven path. And you may come up with a kicker novel. Some have. But don't knock the path of proven success until you try it. You've heard there are no new plot ideas out there, and every story is only a version of ten or so basic plots (or thirty-six dramatic situations, if you go with Georges Polti's view—get his book *The Thirty-Six Dramatic Situations* first published in 1921 but reprinted in 1981, if you can find a copy).

So, determining your protagonist's visible plot goal is the first major element needed to shore up that entrance to your mine shaft. The plot goal will propel your character through the dark scary tunnels, the twists and turns inside the mountain, and will eventually lead straight to the mother lode at the heart of your story.

> Think about . . . playing with your first scenes and decide whether to have your main visible goal be introduced from the start (in the first few pages if possible) or use an inciting incident to throw your protagonist off course and shift him from his initial goal to the real goal of his heart. But keep in mind that the true plot goal is the one your hero will go after all the way to the end of the book, where he will either succeed or fail. That decision is up to you and will be determined by your message or theme.

## Chapter 5: The Major Dramatic Query

*"A prudent question is one half of wisdom."*
~Francis Bacon

You've now learned why the visible "goal" of your protagonist needs to be revealed in some measure in the first few pages, and what we'll explore next is the need to establish what are referred to as the plot question and the spiritual question your book is raising. For, the plot question is tied up in the visible goal (they are pretty much the same thing), but the *spiritual question* is a little different but just as crucial, if not more. Hold on—I'll explain.

You may not have a deeply themed book, but there must be some reason you are writing this story. What is your story about? If you were asked, "Why did you write this book?" (and spend months, maybe years of your life doing so!) how would you answer? Hopefully, there is a specific thing you want to say to your readers.

It doesn't have to be a "message" or sermon on life, but every story deals with themes on one level or another, and your views as a writer will come through the story, sometimes whether you intend it or not. Better to begin a book with intention—intending to say something and leave your readers with that "take-home" thought when they read the last line and close the book. (And we'll be looking more deeply at theme later, but you need to have theme foremost in your mind at the beginning of your novel.)

## Mind Your MDQs

Theme ties in with your MDQ or major dramatic query (or question)—which is the aforementioned "plot question." I think the most important, mind-blowing material I learned in recent years that helped me in my writing craft was to learn about the MDQ. And I hope after you read this you will feel similarly. Now, with every novel I write, I begin with this element. And don't worry, you can learn about MDQ PDQ (pretty darn quickly).

## Yes or No?

The MDQ or major dramatic query is a yes-or-no question you ask at the start of the book. Very simply, it's a question that *must* be addressed in the first scene regarding your protagonist, as it sets the stage for the entire novel. It is also called the visible plot goal (which you have now learned about).

Your question may be "Will Mary save her brother before he kills himself?" or "Will Frodo destroy the ring and save Middle Earth before Sauron gets his hands on it?" or "Will Dorothy make it back to Kansas or be stuck with those annoying munchkins for the rest of her life?" You get the idea. The are only a few variations of this plot question, and they involve the character either getting something or somewhere, saving someone, finding something, or escaping something (as you learned in a previous chapter).

Now, the answer that you reveal at the end of the book can be either yes or no. Maybe Dorothy will, after all, end up living in Munchkinland, but she might enjoy it, and find her true path to happiness there. You're the writer; it's your choice. You *do* have to answer this question, by the way, and that's why you set it up in the first scene. It's the key to your story. But . . . it's not the *heart* of your story.

## The Heart Is in the Spiritual Query

There are actually two sides to this MDQ coin. And now we flip this coin over to find the spiritual query or question. It's a little harder to pinpoint, but it reveals the heart of your character and the heart of your story. Without it, you might have an exciting plot, but will anyone really care about the story, or even read it to the end? Without a spiritual question for your protagonist, the answer may be no.

When I say "spiritual" question, I am not talking about faith or faith-based stories. Every good story has a "spiritual" question that concerns the protagonist. A question that involves the character's spirit—her heart—is what we're concerned with.

Think about Frodo. His MDQ spiritual question might be "Will Frodo find peace and inner contentment through his journey to destroy the ring, even if it kills him in the end?" Dorothy's spiritual question might be "Will Dorothy find her place in the world, feel she fits in, feel at home somewhere?" Think about how these spiritual MDQs are raised at the start of the stories, alongside the plot MDQs. Both questions should be asked in the opening scenes of your novel.

Now, what it crucial to realize is that *both* questions get answered *at the same time and in the same scene* at the end of the book! This is amazing, and when done well, makes your book a winner. Dorothy gets home (plot MDQ) but at the same time she realizes she's always been home; that here, with Aunty Em, is where her heart truly lives (spiritual MDQ). Can't you hear Judy Garland say, "Oh, Aunty Em—there's *no* place like home!" Talk about a clear visible plot goal, with the spiritual MDQ answered metaphorically!

So before you even start writing (or if you are partway through your novel), write down your two MDQs—the plot question and the spiritual question you need to raise in the first scenes that will be answered in one of the last scenes in your book. This is what should shape and give impetus to your entire novel—these questions. Your plot arc and character arcs will all begin and end based on these questions. They seem simple, but the reader needs to know what they are.

This doesn't mean you state them blatantly (although in my novel *Conundrum*, I decided to actually have my main character, Lisa, in first person, ask the MDQ in her head—literally and exactly word for word. That worked for my book, and it sure left no confusion on the reader's part as to what the novel was about and what Lisa's plot and spiritual questions were).

I've given you a lot of important, big things to think about, and I hope you will see how mind-blowing the MDQ topic is!

Think about . . . the MDQ for a while to get the hang of setting up your novel at the start with these important elements. It will make writing your book that much easier. The MDQs become a beacon of light that guides your protagonist on her long, dark journey to the end of the story and into the heart of your story.

# Chapter 6: First Thoughts for Your First Paragraphs

*"Beginnings are always messy."*
~author James Galsworthy

I've been going over all the essential elements you need in your first scene, all of which should show their heads on the first page or two. I've talked about eliminating backstory and excessive explanation and setting up your protagonist's visible plot goals and the MDQs to this point. In this chapter we'll look at a few other essential first-scene elements needed to shore up the structure of your novel and smooth the way to the heart of your story.

If you can succeed at this first scene, you are well on your way to writing a terrific novel. Conversely, if you fail to include *all* the major elements you need right away, you will lose your reader, and that equates to a failed attempt at hooking and keeping your reader turning page after page.

## The #1 Objective for Your Novel

So . . . what is the #1 objective in writing your novel? (Drum roll . . .) To elicit emotion. Not any one specific emotion, but *some* emotion. And you should have an idea of what kind of emotion you'd like to incite in your reader. But that's your aim—to *move* your reader.

Okay, I know I'm veering off course here, but one of my favorite books of all time is Walter Moers's *The City of Dreaming Books.* If you haven't heard of this German author who draws crazy cartoons throughout and has the most wacky, warped imagination on earth, you need to discover him. In this novel, Optimus Yarnspinner, a young writer (who is more like a goofy dragon), inherits from his beloved godfather an unpublished short story by an unknown author. His search for the author's identity takes him to Bookholm—the so-called City of Dreaming Books. On entering its streets, our hero feels as if he has opened the door of a gigantic secondhand bookshop.

Thus begins his journey in the treacherous underground where books are alive, scheming, and intent on trapping and torturing you in catacombs hard to escape. What is so compelling, though, is this short story, which I seem to recall is only ten pages long, is the most spectacular piece of fiction ever written. When Optimus shows it around to the booksellers, they grow obsessive. You watch the fleet of emotions that come across their faces as they read this magnificent piece of work. Tears, shrieks, gasps, cries—it's a masterpiece and unbelievable that anyone could write such stuff. And of course, it then is priceless and highly coveted. Which leads Optimus into all kinds of danger.

My dream is to someday spend a good amount of time (perhaps a year) trying to write the most powerful, beautiful, moving first scene (ten pages) that will evoke this kind of intense emotional response. I hope one day to host a workshop each year called "the Ten-Page Challenge," where a group of writers spend a few days seeing if they can create such a powerful scene. What if you could make your reader cry, become breathless, gasp, experience an elevated heart rate—all this in your first scene. Is it possible? I believe it is.

## First Paragraph, First Thoughts

Since we're discussing the heart of your story and all the major elements you need to set up in your first few pages, I want to stop for a moment and talk about the whole experience of diving in to begin establishing all these essential first elements needed in your novel. As I mentioned earlier, that first scene has a tremendous burden, and you may have to go back once your novel is done and rewrite that scene to tie in neatly with the themes you've developed throughout your novel, as well as homogenize your voice.

There's nothing wrong with this, and if you keep in mind you are just trying to line up all your ducks without too much precision at first, you won't freeze up from the enormous weight of the task. The ducks are going to bump into each other and quack a bit in irritation, but later on you can calm them down and impose order on them so they swim in a nice tidy line. (Okay, just felt like I had to run—paddle?—with that analogy.)

## Who's Your Audience?

I find that I often start each novel a bit rough in terms of voice and style. I don't write each book in the same style; in fact, many of my books showcase such diverse styles that readers have commented that they never would have known I was the author of these very different novels. In a series, for example, you would want to keep the same identifiable voice and style, and that's what I do in my seven-book fantasy series, which I've set up to be able to go deep and evocative with language and imagery. But in my "noir" suspense dramas, I use an entirely different style—more of a tight, terse voice that fits the genre.

And that's what you want to always be thinking about as you begin to write your novel and start setting the tone as you write the first scene. You need to know who your audience is and what style they're expecting when they read that genre. If you're writing strict genre (tailoring your novel to fit in a very specific slot), you need to do your homework and study the style and voice of writers who write those kinds of books. No doubt you are probably already a fan and reader of that genre (that's why you love writing it), and so you should have a feel for this already as you begin your book.

## Where to Start?

In addition to making sure your first scene has all the aforementioned elements, you also want to think about what situation would best set up your premise (what your story is basically about), plot arc, character arc, theme, and mood for your novel. You may have to write a bunch of different first chapters, as I sometimes do. Sometimes it's not until you near the end of writing your book that you get the right idea for the opening scene. You might be like John Irving, who starts every novel with the last line of his book and works backward (yes, he does!). But he's onto something there—do you see?

He knows exactly where he wants his readers *to end up*—plot-wise and theme-wise. He already knows the end of the story and the take-home feeling or thought he wants to evoke, so he sets about figuring how to lead that back to the start. Maybe that technique will work for you.

Think about the heart of your story and the heart of your character. Once you find a way to put her heart right out there from line one, in a scene that throws her at odds with her world and shows how she reacts, you are on your way.

### Introducing Your Character in the Middle of Something

One of the most important decisions you have to make is in picking just the right starting place to begin your novel. You want the story to start in present action, in the middle of something happening, with your POV character right in the situation and revealing her (or his) fears, dreams, needs, or goals and the obstacle that is in the way and presenting a problem.

### What to Focus On

Your voice and style will have a lot of influence on that first scene—the way sentences are structured, the length of the chapter, the tone and pacing. But for the most part, you don't need to concentrate too much on things like pacing and chapter length, for you'll tweak and tighten those in your revisions. What you do want to pay special attention to are the things on the First-Page Checklist. It's a great handy sheet to keep in your notebook next to your desk to refer to as you dig in to your first chapter or come back to rework it.

### Don't Aim for the Mona Lisa

I would suggest you think more about being a sketch artist rather than a detail painter as you write this first chapter. I recall reading an interview with Gabriel Garcia Marquez that so impressed me. In the interview, he mentioned how he often spent months honing the first paragraph of a novel before writing any more, in order to get clear in his head all the major elements he wanted in that book—mostly in regard to tone, voice, pacing, and inciting incident. *One Hundred Years of Solitude* is one of my favorite novels of all time, and his opening paragraph is a great one that does set up all those things for the entire book.

You may be like Marquez and feel you need to labor over that first page for a long while before taking off, but I think for most writers that will only be an exercise in stalling the inevitable—which is to get to work and start writing. Okay, since I've aroused your curiosity, here's his first line: "Many years later, as he faced the firing squad, Colonel Aureliana Buendía was to remember that distant afternoon when his father took him to discover ice." This is a perfect example of introducing a protagonist and jumping into the start of a great scene.

## Use a Pencil; Resist the Eraser

I don't mean this literally, unless you really do like to write your scenes with pad and pencil. What I do mean is that it helps to rough in the first chapter and get the basics down (remember those pesky ducks?), knowing you'll revisit it many times throughout the writing of the novel to tweak it more in line with the developing voice, style, pacing, and themes you draw out and tighten along the way. My first chapters are always a little over-wordy and clunky, and rarely ever start out of the gate with a brilliant hook and opening paragraph. I often come back later and hack about half of that chapter away, or just rewrite the whole thing. But your aim for this first scene should be to get those essential elements in at least in a rough way.

Think about . . . a novel you've read that had an amazing, powerful first chapter. It may not have the punch that Optimus's special story had, but no doubt you can think of some novel that got you so excited you dropped everything to keep reading. If you can get a hold of that book and reread the chapter, then pay special attention to the details and elements that so moved you. Think how you can do something similarly in your first scene. Jot your observations down in your notebook.

Whether you're just beginning your novel or have a first or second draft you're working on, think about your audience and how the tone and style of writing is suited (or not) to that readership.

# Chapter 7: The Hook of the First Paragraph

*"The whole point is to hook people and keep them interested."*
~actress Penelope Miller

We're now continuing our look at the rest of the items listed on the First-Page Checklist. Some of these elements will be explored in greater detail in later chapters, but because they need to show up in your first scene or two, we'll go over them a bit to be sure you understand what they are and how to present them so they will lead to the heart of your story.

I'm going to hear some groans and objections when I say there are three things that really should not only be in your first scene but specifically *in your first paragraph.* You can't always do this, but if you can, you are starting your story off with a bang.

## Three Things You Should Have in Your Novel's First Paragraph

That first paragraph is probably going to be the hardest one to write and polish since it carries the biggest burden in your novel (and the last paragraph in the book carries the second biggest burden). It's fine to just throw something out there to get started, knowing you'll come back and make it much better. But before you can write that first paragraph, you should know what your first scene is going to be about—and it has to be about some specific things:

- *Your protagonist.* Unless you are writing a prologue (if you really must) that involves some other characters, you want that first scene to showcase your protagonist. Why? Because you are clueing your reader to pay attention to this particular character right from the start. Your readers will assume the first character they are introduced to, with the scene being told in his POV (point of view), *is* your protagonist and the one they will want to root for. There are exceptions to this, of course, but as a general rule, this is the time-tested and best way to start.

- *A catalyst or incident.* Your opening scene should start off with a bang, with your protagonist in the middle of something that we sense has been going on for a while. Insinuate a conflict, a problem, some tense situation that puts the protagonist right in the heart of a scene that will be the perfect milieu to showcase her humanity, needs, fears, dreams, or whatever it is you want to reveal about her to the reader at the start. This incident or situation should provide a great platform for your MDQ and plot goal. This is why you need to spend some serious time thinking about the setting, locale, and situation of your first scene.

- *A hint of the protagonist's core need.* This is essential. Basically, you want to introduce a character who has a visible goal (as we've gone over)—but what does that translate to? That she has a need. Hence, the reason she has a goal. If Indiana Jones's goal is to get the Ark of the Covenant, it's because he has a need. Now, in a different story, his need may be to get enough money to pay the rent and what is *motivating* him is his desire not to be homeless, so he's driven by a need to survive by going after a reward. Or his need could be for fame, for humanitarian purposes, to impress a girl—the list is endless. It's your story, so you should know *why* your protagonist wants to reach that visible goal. So hint at what that is. Even though that visible goal may not be clearly

> established until the 25 percent mark of your novel, that first paragraph needs to begin setting up the need that will be the core motivation for that goal.

Now, I'm not suggesting you have to write a three-page first paragraph to get all this in there. In fact, that first paragraph may tell us very little and just give us a great hook and introduce your character in some compelling situation (at very least you need that). But you do need all this on your first page—at least a hint of this. It's doable—really! And essential to the heart of your story.

## Hook 'Em on the First Cast

If you look at your First-Page Checklist, you'll see that the first three elements I just discussed—introduction of your protagonist, a catalyst or incident to put her in that showcases her, and a hint of her core need (linked to her visible plot goal)—actually cover a few more things on the checklist. I haven't talked about the hook, and rather than thumb through some great novels and give you a long list, I would encourage you to do that and think about how effective these first lines are. But I will give you a couple of "catchy hooks" (sorry about the pun) that stick out in my mind (below).

## Hook, Line, and Sinker

What is a hook all about anyway? It's a line that snags your reader and pulls him into the story. Often someone flipping through your book or looking at the first page online at Amazon.com will read just the first few lines. I have heard agents and acquisition editors say that they will pretty much decide to either stop or continue reading based on that first sentence, or possibly the first paragraph. Yikes! So, that first line should be a doozy and one that really makes an impression.

As I said before, don't get so hung up on writing that first paragraph that you don't move forward. You will probably come back and rewrite it, unless you came up with an opening line ages ago and now you're finally putting that bit of brilliance in place. Sometimes as we're writing our novel a great first line will come to us. Other times we'll find a great first line somewhere on page three or four. When I went back in after completing one of my recent novels to chop away at my boring, extra-long first chapter (and this is usually the only chapter I do this with), I found a catchy, compelling first line on page two. I pretty much eliminated everything before it and started there.

It doesn't matter when you come up with that great first line, but, in the end, you will want a terrific one—and you should not settle for less. Your reader will expect it.

## A Couple of Great First Lines

That first line should be intriguing, and if it doesn't specifically name your protagonist, it should have a feel of being in her POV and something that's important to her. I keep thinking of Harry Dolan's first novel *Bad Things Happen* (that won one of the Amazon Breakthrough Novel Award contests). This is a suspense novel with intrigue and murder in a stylized voice that is refreshing and wonderful. Here's the first line: "The shovel has to meet certain requirements."

As you can see, it doesn't introduce the protagonist, but it arouses curiosity. Why in the world is a novel opening with the discussion of a shovel? What will it be used for? The next lines in the first paragraph answer that question . . . to a point (pardon my pun): "A pointed blade. A short handle to make it maneuverable in a small space. He finds what he needs in the gardening section of a vast department store."

Of course, the reader has read the blurb on the back cover so knows what the book is about and what the genre is. This type of opening is perfect for Dolan's audience: mystery-suspense readers looking for something a bit noir or macabre. I think this is a great hook because it is full of microtension—meaning, it raises your curiosity and gets you to wonder about this character and why he needs a shovel. Obviously the shovel must be important, and we suspect it will be used for something creepy and not related to gardening. And off we go, reading on.

Another great first line comes from *The Lovely Bones* by Alice Sebold. This story is told in first person, so it automatically introduces the protagonist through her voice. "My name was Salmon, like the fish; first name, Susie." What the reader catches right away is the past tense: My name *was* Salmon. What? Did she change her name? You find out in the next line: "I was fourteen when I was murdered on December 6, 1973." Right away we're intrigued, as we realize this story is being told by a girl who is dead—and not just dead but murdered.

How about Richard Matheson's great first line in *I am Legend*: "On those cloudy days, Robert Neville was never sure when sunset came, and sometimes they were in the streets before he could get back." Here's a perfect example of what I advised earlier stating what writers should have in that first paragraph (or sentence): an introduction of the protagonist, showing something of a conflict or inciting incident, and the character's core need. Need I say more?

Keep in mind, then, that the opening hook may require two or three sentences. But don't stretch it. A hook is a quick snag, not a long haul. The shorter and catchier you can make it, the better.

Think about . . . looking at your first paragraph and seeing if you have all three things listed above in there. Or at very least on your first page. However, the closer to the first paragraph you can get with these elements, the sooner you will grab your reader. Pull out a few of your favorite novels or thumb through some books at the bookstore and read the first paragraph. See if some of those best sellers have these elements in the first paragraph, and examine the ones that really catch your attention. Why do they work? Play around with your novel's first line. If you have a few you are toying with, throw them out to some friends of family members to get a reaction. Maybe that will help you hone it so it's just the right opening line for your book.

## Chapter 8: A Few More First-Scene Essentials

*"Words mean more than what is set down on paper.*
*It takes the human voice to infuse them with deeper meaning."*
~Maya Angelou

Because I will be going into more detail in part two about characters—who are truly the heart of your story—I only briefly want to touch on the necessity of giving something to your reader in this first scene to make him "like your protagonist," as it's listed on the First-Page Checklist. Regardless of whether your novel follows a hero/heroine type or a "dark protagonist" (a negative character, which is very popular these days in paranormal and urban fantasy novels), you really do need to make him likeable or empathetic.

Many manuscripts I critique show protagonists who are very unappealing or abrasive. They say and do nothing that makes me care for them; to the contrary, they often make me dislike them so much by the end of the first scene that I would never continue reading the book if I wasn't paid to do so. The argument I get from writers who feature these types of characters is they want to show their character starting out as someone unlikeable and needing to change or be redeemed or have an epiphany by the end of the book.

Sure, we do want our characters to grow and change, but unless you somehow show something appealing about them, or show a glimmer of their potential to be "great," you will lose your reader long before you get a chance to show the wonderful changes he is making. I will be going into much greater detail as to how to show that "glimpse of greatness" in your first scene, but keep in mind you will need to have this element somewhere in your first scene.

## Setting and Theme

Two additional elements listed on the checklist is a nod to setting and conveying your theme. Both will be covered in later chapters, but for now, keep in mind that you will need to somehow establish your setting to your reader in a concise, appropriate way (appropriate to the genre and your style of writing, avoiding long passages of boring description).

Because theme is such an important part of the heart of your story, I am devoting a whole section of the book to it. Although it is not mentioned on the First-Page Checklist, it is an essential element that should be present throughout your novel, and should be at least hinted at in some way in your first scene.

## Watch Your Tone

Since you need to establish the tone of your book right from the start, I want to spend a little bit of time discussing this element. Tone is a subtle thing, and it overlaps sound, style, and voice (which I'll explain after this part on tone). Whereas voice is really generated and inspired by your characters, tone is something more consistent and covers your whole book. Kind of like icing spread over the top of a multi-flavor cake—the voice of all your characters being the different flavors.

## Give a Feel for How You Feel

Tone really has nothing to do with how you construct a sentence, paragraph, or even chapter. Think of tone as your (the author's) overall opinion or feeling about your story. Maybe this is confusing, but when you think of the story you are writing, what emotional attitudes come into play? Sarcasm, humor, cynicism, anger, jubilation? If you're telling a story about oppression and cruelty, is it because you feel passionately about this topic and want people to be moved to take a particular stand? Your tone should reflect this.

Of course, this doesn't mean your tone should be inciting a riot. What it does mean is your writing style will convey this feeling you have. Your sentences and scenes will have an undercurrent of seriousness, poignancy, or perhaps intensity. In contrast, if you are writing a lighthearted adventure story, your tone may express humor, flippancy, even a bit of obnoxiousness. What you want is to give a feel for how *you* feel.

Tone is subjective. It may seem like it's the same as voice, but it's not. When I think of Kurt Vonnegut's novels, I can sense his cynical tone splashed with outrageous humor as an undercurrent beneath his voice. Same with Tom Robbins. So, since tone is subjective (implying there's an author out there with an opinion), you do want to be careful your tone doesn't come across haughty, know-it-all, pompous, etc. It's fine to have a *character* who is pompous, but you don't want the tone of your novel to be pompous.

I hope you can see the difference. I see some first novels in which the author has worked really hard to use as many fancy, eccentric, and never-used words as they can in order to impress their readers (sorry, they're not impressed—just irritated). In those cases, the tone of the book gets in the way of the story being told.

## Separate Your Tone from Your Characters' Voices

Now, if you write a book in the first-person POV of a brilliant statesman and he's telling the story, even though his voice will sound pompous (perhaps), the tone of the book should not. In his thoughts and speech he may use big words, but you as the writer would construct your sentences without all those flowery words. You would build your sentences influenced by how you feel about this character and the story you are telling. That way the *tone* of that novel will be *your* subjective tone—not the character's. If this character is a dark, evil man who did horrible crimes against humanity, your tone will be serious, intense, maybe even a bit objective to give distance and let the reader feel what she may. I hope the tone of this section reflects my interest in giving you insight and writing skills!

## Where's My Voice?

So, if that is tone, what is an author's "voice"? This term is discussed in countless books, websites, and anywhere writing is taught. It seems like a nebulous thing. Just what is voice? How can you tell when an author "has it" and when she doesn't? What should a voice sound like as it relates to the novel you are writing?

I don't want to go into a lengthy thesis about voice, and there are so many schools of thought on this. So, I'll just focus on two key points that make the most sense to me.

- Be honest and courageous: The more you try to copy books that are out there and sound like authors you are trying to emulate, the more derivative you are going to sound. There's something forced and phony that comes across when you try to write like someone else and not yourself. So part of what voice is is a measure of honesty and a courage to be yourself as you write. Okay, that sounds vague too, but over time, the more you write, the more you will find your voice coming out and asserting itself. I think the whole topic of voice is very subjective, and all I can tell you is what I really like in a novel (as far as voice goes) and what works for me as I write (in terms of developing a voice for that particular book).

- Think more about giving your *characters* voice rather than trying to come up with an author voice: If you are writing in first person, this is really essential and obvious. You are going to be in that one character's head the entire novel, and so you want to spend time getting to know your character. How does she think, talk, respond to others? Where did she grow up and when? All the factors of a character's background affect how she thinks and reacts to her world. And this comes out in voice as she internalizes and processes things that happen to her from one scene to the next. In third person, you can do pretty much the same by using a deep POV that feels a whole lot like first-person POV.

## Try Writing As If You Were a Dog

If you don't really get how you can come up with a unique voice that fits your story, try writing some thoughts or create a little scene, but take the point of view of a dog. Garth Stein did this beautifully in a novel that's one of my all-time favorites: *The Art of Racing in the Rain.* I love Enzo and feel he is a very human character with a truly human voice even though he's a dog. Maybe you can rewrite one of your scenes from the mind of a cat, having the cat tell what's happening and remarking on how he feels about the way those humans are behaving around him (I've edited two great novels from cats' POVs). Okay, if you're a chicken lover, go with the chicken voice. I actually have a number of friends who are in love with their pet chickens. Go figure. (And these last few sentences should give you a good feel for both my tone and my voice in this passage of the book.)

If you play with voice like this, it might help you realize that each character will have a personality that comes out in and by their voice. And that voice becomes the voice of your novel. If you have multiple POV characters, they should each have a different and unique voice.

Voice is really about letting your characters loose. Let them emote and react and tell you how they feel about what's going on. If you get out of the way and let them take center stage, I think you'll find the voice will present itself. That's been my experience.

Think about . . . taking a look at the tone of your novel so far and see if you are getting across the subjective mood you intend. Take a look at some other novels and see if you can determine what the tone is. For fun, try writing your first scene in the point of view of some other character or animal. If you are writing in third person, try first person for your protagonist. Or put the scene in a secondary character's POV and hear how she talks as she sees the scene unfold.

## Getting (Honest) Feedback

Hopefully by now you've written that first scene and you really like it! If you feel you've polished it and it now has every essential element present, you'll want to give it to some people to read. No, not your mom or spouse or best friend. You need to find some other authors, and preferably ones with some editing chops. Or if you want to be sure you're getting really helpful feedback, hire a professional copyeditor and writing coach. I edit and judge (for contests) a lot of first scenes, and I've yet to read one that doesn't have me writing extensive comments on just about every page. That doesn't mean I'm so picky and critical I can't give praise. What I'm saying is that it's really hard to see if you've covered all those bases and created a riveting first scene that will stand out from the piles of manuscripts competing for an agent's attention.

I know you're probably thinking I'm only trying to drum up business for myself here, but I try to get *my* manuscripts critiqued and read by readers who have these chops and will spare no barbs. I don't want to put out a weak novel, and I'd rather have my test readers tear the thing apart and catch every mistake and plot hole *now* so I don't have to cringe once the book is in print and I find I did some stupid stuff (or have readers point them out, which some are most glad to do).

So, even if you're happy with your critique team, consider running a few chapters by a professional writing coach with experience in critiquing novels. After that, you can certainly hire a proficient copyeditor to correct your spelling and grammatical mistakes. But don't just send your novel out on submission or self-publish it without putting it through a bit of fire. Fire serves some good purposes. When you put impure silver through the fire, all the scummy dross rises to the surface. That's a good thing, because you can then skim it all off and you're left with something in its purest, finest state.

## Critiques May Hurt for a Moment but . . .

If you can get past the ego and insecurity issues tied up in having others critique your work, your manuscript will be better for it. And you'll be much happier with it once you make the needed changes. It doesn't mean you have to make every correction an editor suggests, but if you take to heart all that's said and be teachable, you will grow as a writer and write better each year. There's nothing more satisfying than holding your published novel in your hand knowing you polished it; had it critiqued and edited; and wrote a beautiful, coherent story.

And this wraps up our look at first scenes.

Think about . . . going over the First-Page Checklist and see if you've left anything out. If you feel your chapter (or novel) is done, consider having a professional take a look at it and give you feedback. Or have the first fifty pages critiqued. Believe me, once you get those pages critiqued, you will have a whole new, clear focus and understanding of the big picture. Talk to friends who've hired editors and get recommendations.

If you're not ready, gear your mind and heart to accept that at some point it might be a good thing to let someone else look at what you've written and give you advice. We can all improve, every one of us—best-selling author, writing teacher—everyone.

We have now covered all the basic elements on the First-Page Checklist, but there is more—so much more—that has to be present and aiming at the heart of your story in your opening pages. And the greatest tool needed to mine the heart of your story is your characters.

# Part Two: The Heart of Your Characters

## Chapter 9: Characters Are Everything

*"Action, reaction, motivation, emotion all have to come from the characters."*
~Nora Roberts

Since this book is all about helping writers get to the heart of their stories, there is nothing more important than character, for your protagonist *is* at the heart of the story. Yep, that's my opinion, and you are free to disagree. There are plenty of readers and writers out there who believe plot is the all-important consideration. They feel if a plot is terrific and compelling, the characters can be weak, superficial, stereotyped, and uninteresting. They feel the plot will be so engaging—yes, even riveting—the reader won't care a hoot who populates their story. And maybe there are a bunch of novels selling well (praised by a myriad of faithful readers) that really are structured like this.

Fine, I say. But I'll add this: I doubt any of those novels have *heart* or speak to the reader's heart in such a way to move them emotionally or affect them or their lives in any significant way. And the writer of that type of book may say, "So what?" They aren't intending to reach the heart. But perhaps you are—that's why you are reading this book. Because you don't want to write a forgettable book.

I will be so bold as to say that the *only* way you are going to write that powerful, memorable, breathtakingly beautiful book is if you have terrific complex, rich, and unique characters. Creating such characters takes work, and these chapters will show you how to get to the heart of your characters.

Yes, a great plot is essential to a great book, and I can't stand plot holes and loose ends in the novels I read and edit. Plot is important—you'll get no argument from me on that issue. But a plot without great characters is like . . . well, a book with blank pages. You get to the end and feel nothing. And when I read a novel, I really want to feel something—a lot of things. I want to be moved emotionally, and the way that happens is by being pulled into the characters in the story and made to care what happens to them. Author Jeffrey Deaver sums it up this way: "My books are primarily plot-driven, but the best plot in the world is useless if you don't populate them with characters that readers can care about."

So, with that said, let's dive into the heart of your characters—see what makes them tick . . . and laugh and cry and yell.

## Ordinary People Are Just Plain Boring

I want to talk a little about the introduction of your protagonist, since that is on the First-Page Checklist, and I only touched on character in the first part of this book. The opening of your book presents a crucial moment that gives a first glimpse or impression of your main character. You know what they say about first impressions—they tend to stick with you and are hard to erase. If someone rubs you the wrong way when you meet them, it's sometimes hard to get past that initial feeling. It almost feels a bit embedded in concrete.

So it is with your characters as they walk upon the stage of your novel. If you're at a party and you meet someone dull and completely unappealing, you're not likely to pay much attention to them from that point on. The same is true with your characters. You don't want them to come across boring. Of course, if you need a character to be a bore, make them an interesting one. The point is to always make your characters a bit larger than life.

Perhaps you're thinking you want your protagonist to be an average "everyman" type of guy—that way the reader will be able to relate to him, right? Wrong. Who wants to read about uninteresting, average people? No one. Sure, we want to be able to relate in some ways to your protagonist, but we are reading to be engaged, entertained, enthralled. And a boring, flat character is not going to incite those feelings in us.

So, how do you create a sympathetic, intriguing character that is not a raving lunatic and be able to get the reader to care about her on the first page? It takes some planning and thinking ahead to pull this off. And believe me, a lot of readers are going to lose interest by page three if you haven't given them a good reason to care. That's why we put our protagonists in a present-action situation that allows us to reveal a bit about the heart of our character. As discussed in earlier chapters, we have to point to the visible goal of the character right away, but we also need to *see* her heart.

## Create an Immediate Bond

Donald Maass, in his great book *The Fire in Fiction*, says that to "create an immediate bond between reader and protagonist, it is necessary to show your reader a reason to care." And to do that, he says we have to show a "glimpse of greatness."

Just what does that mean? Our protagonist may not be all that great; in fact, he may be a real loser. Again—would we want to keep reading about a loser? We might . . . if we see he has a glimpse of greatness. All this means is that you show a piece of this character that is heroic—which can be translated into many things, like noble, virtuous, passionate about something significant, humanitarian, self-sacrificing, or some other attractive quality that pulls us toward him.

And this doesn't mean you have to open with a scene where the loser jumps overboard and saves a drowning child in a huge storm at sea. That might come later, near the climax of your novel. What it does mean is that somewhere in that first scene, and preferably in the first page or two, you will want to show (not tell) your character doing and/or saying something that makes us think he's got something redeeming and special about him.

## Greatness

Greatness doesn't mean a person is great. You can have a sympathetic, dark, brooding character—a negative protagonist—that's going to change and become an amazing person at the end of the book. But you can't expect your readers to trust that you'll get him there if you don't give a glimpse of his potential at the outset. If you have a dark protagonist, show that he's not happy being this way, that he wants to change.

Here's an insightful thing to remember: *A great character is not shown by who they are but by the impact they have on others.* So think *impact.* What can you have your character be doing as the book opens that will allow the reader to see that your protagonist might have the *potential* to affect change (on others)? Maass says, "Great people do not leave the world unchanged."

Think about . . . some great characters you love. You can surely think of great characters in literature and current novels that have really worked their way into your heart. If you have any of those books on hand (or you can usually preview a portion online at Amazon.com), read the first page or two and note the place(s) where the author was able to convey this greatness in her protagonist. If you go through and study many well-written novels, you will start getting an idea of how to subtly and simply show a glimpse of greatness. And that is exactly what you need to get your reader to care.

## Chapter 10: The Essence and Persona of Character

*"Heart is what drives us and determines our fate. That is what I need for my characters in my books: a passionate heart."*
~author Isabel Allende

While we're going deep into character, and most importantly, your protagonist, I want to add in some insights and prod your thinking about the aspects of your character's personality. Writing instructor and screenwriter Michael Hague enriches the traditional three-act structure (his is a six-act structure) by overlaying the progressive journey of the protagonist. I found his take quite eye-opening, for although I understood the concept of a character portraying himself to the world one way while underneath he's really a different person at heart, I never thought about the process of revealing this "inner man" until I took a workshop from him.

### Persona vs. Essence

All of us are flawed. Over the years, since childhood, we have developed a "face" we present to the world. Often that face is formed by hurts we've suffered early on. We start out all innocent and sweet, and then after a few of life's hard knocks, we hide behind a persona that feels safe. A true hero's journey will show the process of the hero moving from his persona to his true essence by the end of the story. And this is a great model for novelists.

Almost all great stories show the protagonist at the start of the book in his normal world. This is the place in which he functions, interacts with others, and makes his way through life. And this has him "showing his persona" to the world as well—the person he *wants* others to think he is.

But if you're telling a rich story, there's going to be something wrong with this picture. Even if this character seems happy, we can tell he's really not. There is something missing in his life—and that's because he's not really being his true self—the person he really wants to be and is deep inside.

This feature of your character doesn't have to do with his visible goal established early on in the book. Oh, they are interconnected, of course, and the goal should be a vehicle for helping your character "find himself." But although he may believe this, his reaching his visible goal isn't the real thing that will make him truly happy. Every person who is not living in his or her "true essence" is going to be unhappy (even if they think they're happy) until they come into their essence—who they really are.

So, your character should reveal this in the first chapter somewhere. Not that they're miserable and glum. You can have a really happy character step onto the stage. What I'm talking about here is showing some aspect of the character's persona (the face he presents to the world) that is not really him, not how he truly feels, and is the source of some dissatisfaction in his life because, well, he's being phony in at least some way.

### Who Really Is My Hero?

Here's a question you can ask: "Who would my hero be if he could really find the courage to [or was forced to] strip away his outward personality and reveal his true self?" A great story hints *at the start* of the novel that the protagonist *has the potential* to be something else, something better, something more true. Notice I say "hints" and "potential." You don't have to hit the reader over the head with a psychosis that is making your character plum crazy. We all, for the most part, live day in and day out with our "minor" neuroses due to the way we were raised or the tough knocks we've had to endure in life. Sometimes we will go through life fairly functional without ever noticing how screwed up we are or having the urge to change (I'll be the first to put up my hand).

But readers don't want to read about *those* kinds of people. They want to see a character change, grow, learn, make life-altering decisions. What they really want is to see your character move from her persona to her essence by the end of the book. Really. So think about who your hero or heroine would really be if they could truly be the person they really want to be.

This ties in with the last chapter's section on showing a glimpse of greatness. Readers love to see something redeemable in humanity. Even with the darkest of antagonists, there's nothing richer and more engaging than seeing a human, authentic side. Think Darth Vader. So, the journey of your hero from start to finish in the story would be one of him starting fully in his persona and ending in a place where he embraces and lives fully in his true essence.

## Shrek Is Really Not Who He Thinks He Is

Hague uses Shrek as the perfect example of this journey. Shrek presents himself to the world as a mean ogre. That's how he survives. He denies his softer side because it has not served him well in the past, and he believes it's a weakness. But by the end of the movie, after he's been having to face his essence and battle with embracing it, he finally breaks through to becoming his true self—a really goodhearted, loving ogre with honor and a kind heart.

Stories with characters who grow in this manner really move us. And since we're talking about the heart of the story, you may want to consider this overarching process for your protagonist. If you do, you need to set up in that first scene a glimpse not only of his persona and the face he presents in his normal present world but that glimpse of greatness and true essence—which he might not even see or acknowledge at all. But the *reader* needs to see it.

Think about . . . novels and movies you've seen in which the protagonist at the beginning is in his or her persona and not thriving, but then by the end of the movie has changed. There are hundreds of them out there, and that's because this is a structure that resonates with us and one we love. Some I can think of right away are *The Firm, You've Got Mail,* (well, just about any chick flick*!*), *Liar, Liar*, and Dickens's *A Christmas Carol.*

## Chapter 11: Creating Not Good but Great Characters

*"I imagine that my characters have become much more complicated than when I first began, which would be normal."*

~Irwin Shaw

In this book, I don't want to get into the nuts and bolts of developing characters. There are plenty of online websites and blogs that have lessons in coming up with characters and how to make them seem real and not like wood posts. What I do want to explore, though, is a deeper and more personal approach to developing the characters in your novel.

I've heard various authors speak and teach on how to come up with characters for your novel. Some flip through magazines and cut out pictures, then paste them onto a sheet of paper and write up a bio. Others use tools such as the Myers-Briggs personality chart to create character profiles. Some think of actors they like and just plug them in as characters in their novel. My feeling is if that works for you, then great. There isn't one surefire way to create a great character. But I'd like to share some thoughts I have on the topic, now that I've written more than a dozen novels and they're all "character-driven."

## Write What You Know

I believe that if we tap into the things we love and hate about characters and their traits, we're really telling a lot about ourselves. Some interviewers at times ask me if I "put myself" into my novels. There's a reason that's a common question—we write about what we know. And for the most part, we know ourselves. We know what we like about people and what we don't like. And most psychologists will tell you that those are the very things we like and dislike about ourselves.

I would say "Author, know thyself." When we get honest with ourselves about our shortcomings as well as good qualities, we find a rich mix of character within us. People are complex and sometimes contradictory. I am full of surprises—to myself at times (and often to my disappointment). Writers sometimes feel they must create a character that is wholly predictable and consistent, but we're not really like that.

## Real People are Complex and Contradictory

People change all the time. Maybe not their core beliefs, but their opinions and attitudes may waver from moment to moment based on the mood, who's influencing them at the time, whether they skipped lunch, or missed their daily dose of coffee. One day I may think cats are awful and the next day, after meeting Rex with the best purr and sweetest demeanor, I've become a cat lover.

I know I'm a picky editor and reader. It takes a lot for you to get me to love your characters. It takes a lot for you to get me to believe they're real, three-dimensional, deep, complex. That's what I yearn for when I read a novel—great characters. It's as if I thirst for them, and if the pages flip by and I'm not engaged by the characters (even if the plot is fantastic), I tend to give up. I often give up reading a novel by page two. I've done it a lot, and it's almost always after reading the first few paragraphs in the character's POV and finding they are flat, stereotypic, boring, predictable, and often just plain unlikeable.

## Take the Time—A Lot of Time

I talked in earlier chapters how to get your reader to care about your protagonist right away by showing a glimpse of greatness and by revealing their visible goal. That's all well and good (and needed). But a first scene does not a whole novel make. Before you even start that first scene, I would suggest—no, urge—you to spend some lengthy time working on your characters. Readers want to love (and hate) the characters in your novel, so it is vital you take the time *in advance* to bring them to life. If you've already written your novel and your test readers are telling you your characters are flat, stereotyped, or don't interest them, then maybe some of these techniques and approaches I'm going to present shortly will help.

> Think about . . . a few great characters in novels you've read lately. Think about why you think they're great. If you want to do some hard work that you'll benefit from, go through a novel that has great characters and either underline (if you don't mind desecrating books—I do it all the time) or jot down on paper or in your notebook lines that reveal a character's different qualities, beliefs, feelings, traits. Study how these descriptions have formed a rich picture of who this person is and why they seem so real to you. The more real a character is to the reader, the more emotion that character can evoke.

## Chapter 12: Getting to the Core of Your Characters

*"All the great writers root their characters in true human behaviour."*
~Ben Kingsley

Leon Surmelian in his book (written forty years ago) *Techniques of Fiction Writing* has this to say about creating characters in fiction: "Characterization is a complex and elusive art and cannot be reduced to exact rules or to a comprehensive statement. The more we talk about it, the more we feel has been left out, and this is necessarily so because the human personality remains a mystery, subject to obscure forces; it is a universe in itself, and we are strangers even to ourselves…Characterization requires self-knowledge, insight into human nature…it is more than impersonation."

### Getting Real Doesn't Happen on Its Own

That quote contains some terrific stuff. Too many characters are just that—impersonations of real people. In order to create really *real* characters, you have to be somewhat of a psychologist and learn about human nature. Suffice it to say, many of the novels I read fall short on creating real characters. And I don't think it's only due to not spending enough time working on them. I sense that some authors spend a whole lot of time thinking about their characters, but their creations still come across flat and stereotyped. It may have something to do with laziness and not wanting to work too hard to create each character. It may be that the writer doesn't think characters have to be all that developed—that as the plot unfolds, the character will just "come into his own" and become real. I'm thinking, though, the real reason is the writer hasn't gone deep into herself and examined why she is who *she* is.

I'm not suggesting we all go into therapy for a while or spend years psychoanalyzing ourselves (although some of us writers might benefit from that). But if we do some digging inside, we'll find there are certain truths about why we are the way we are. And the first idea I'd like to throw out at you is tied in with what I wrote earlier about persona and true essence.

Remember, we all present a face to the world—a face we feel will help us survive—which is not wholly who we are. Some people may really live in that place of "true essence," and that's great. But populating a novel with characters like that only gives us "happy people in happy land" (as author James Scott Bell likes to say). Readers are more interested in flawed characters, and I bet, if you're like me, there are some serious flaws lingering under the surface.

## Getting to Know You

So, I'm going to share one technique I use when I sit down to create my characters for a novel. I already at this point have my characters in mind. I know my plot and premise, and I either may already have a lot of the story worked out, or I might have only a germ of an idea. It doesn't matter. But at some point I will sit down (for numerous days) and spend time creating the characters that are going to be the heart and blood of my novel. This time spent is crucial to me, and I never begin writing a novel until my characters are so well fleshed out that I know pretty much everything I need to know about them. And I'm not talking about what they like to eat or what movies they watch. That stuff is inconsequential—trust me. Those little bits about character that come out in your novel are only coloring, not meat.

Most of my novels have up to a dozen main POV characters, so every one of them must be totally real—to me. I don't let them run off and start behaving without getting to that place first. I can't stress enough how vital it is you do this in advance of writing your book. Some writers think it's fine to just start writing and let the characters run amok to see what they'll do. That's all well and good if writing to you is mostly an expression of spontaneity and creativity.

However, if you want to write a very specific story and convey very specific themes, this isn't going to work. Some writers are truly brilliant and can pull this off. Maybe you can, but I can't. So I have to do a bit of work to make my characters really come alive.

## The Three Most Important Things!

I write down my list of main characters on a page. Or sometimes I'll do this on the first page of my character sketches (not actual drawings but thoughts and ideas on them). Then I spend some time thinking about these things:

- Their core need (and what they would do if they couldn't get that need met)
- Their greatest fear
- The incident(s) that wounded them early in life that got them believing a lie about themselves (and/or the world).

These three points are so helpful and powerful that it's just possible they are all you need to create each character. If you learn only *one* thing from this book on writing the heart of your story, then make it this tip. Tape these three points to your wall if you need to remember them! The last point is the most crucial and the one I spend the most time with.

Each of us has been hurt in the past. Because of that hurt, two things resulted:

- We created a false front to protect our heart. Like the girl who was abandoned by her father when she was young and now can't get close to men or stay in a relationship long. If you look at yourself, you will find something in there like this. Somewhere in your past you got hurt, and so you've formed a persona to survive in the world.

- That hurt makes us believe a lie about ourselves and the world. In this example, the lie this girl believes is that all men walk out and always will. That she can't trust men or

> give her heart to them. And that's why her whole life she's kept her distance. That's the outward lie. The other side to that lie turns inward (and you need to look at both parts—they are two sides of the same coin). That part says something about yourself. With this example, the girl believes a lie about *herself*—that she's not worthy of being loved.

**Need = Fear = Lie (Repeat)**

Ah, do you see that? That's rich, deep, powerful. Okay, that character type is used a lot, especially in chick flicks, but I hope you can see here how we're getting to the heart of motivation. Think: when you put this girl in various scenes, she is going to react certain ways based on the lies she's been telling herself her whole life and the lies she believes about other people. This then ties in with her greatest fear (fear of intimacy, fear of abandonment) and her core need, which is . . . have you guessed it?

See the connection? Her core need is to get *the very thing she believes is impossible* because of the lies she believes. She wants more than anything to be loved, but she can't get there. She's blocking her own way. Your character's greatest need should be intrinsically tied in with the lie she believes and her greatest fear (which is not getting that need met). If it sounds simple, it really is. It's our human condition.

The core need generates the fear (of not getting that need met). And at the heart of that fear is the ingrained lie. The journey to the heart of your character is the process of her coming to understand and overcome the lie that has held her in fear.

> Think about . . . looking at your protagonist and examining those three core points. Write a page or two exploring his or her needs, fears, and the lies believed. If you're on a roll, go at it with all your main and even secondary characters.

# Chapter 13: Ordinary Characters Can Be Extraordinary

*"I think it's just that when characters are given enough texture and backbone, then lo and behold, they stand on their own."*

~Anne Tyler

We've been going deep into character these last chapters, and I want to offer you some more ideas for developing complex, riveting characters. We hear things like "Your characters need to be larger than life," meaning they should be extraordinary (extra ordinary? A whole lot more ordinary than the next guy? Sorry, that word got me thinking about how counterintuitive the word is). Okay, I get that to a point. To me, that means they need to be complex, unique, passionate about something.

But I would like to say you can have ordinary characters that are ordinary people, but what makes them engaging and believable is their complex issues that drive them. For we all have them. You could say we are all both ordinary and extraordinary people. If I'm presented one way, I can seem very dull, boring, average. But if I'm presented another way, I can become compelling, fascinating, deep. It's all in the presentation. And in tightly developing and understanding those three essential aspects I spoke of in the last chapter: knowing the character's core need, their deepest fear, and the lie they tell themselves because of the wound they suffered early on. I like the way actor Edward Norton puts it: "All people are paradoxical. No one is easily reducible, so I like characters who have contradictory impulses or shades of ambiguity."

## The Superficial Stuff is Superficial

If you start with those elements and get them richly drawn, you can then move on to other aspects of your character. The problem I see is most writers think the way you identify and distinguish one character from another is by outward things: appearance, hairstyle, dress, manner of talking, etc., so they put these characters in their story and what readers encounter is a lot of description about them that only pertains to outward things. There's a paragraph on how they look, the color of their eyes and hair, what they're eating, and the things they talk about—which are shallow. Well, for good reason. These are the only things the author has spent time developing. And frankly, when I read a novel, the last thing I care about is the protagonist's hairstyle. Now, with a book like *The Devil Wears Prada*, you have to be all about appearances. But even so, to have a great story and engaging characters, you would need to get under all that hair and makeup to find the not-so-beautiful person beneath who has needs and fears, and believes lies.

Before I go on to some other techniques and suggestions on how to create great characters, let me give you a few examples of how I thought up these things for my main characters in one of my novels *in relation to the needs of the plot.* Also, having a little understanding of psychology helps, and if you don't know much about—for example—family dynamics, you can read up on it.

In the family saga novel I wrote titled *Intended for Harm*, I had nine family members I tracked over a forty-year period. My novel is a modern retelling of the Bible story of Jacob and his son Joseph, and it has many themes. The main theme revolves around the protagonist, Jacob, which is all about his bad relationship with his father and the type of father he becomes to his own sons. You could say, in general, my theme is about fathers and sons, and how sons repeat the "sins" of their fathers.

So I knew Jacob's big lie stemmed from the hurt meted out by an unloving father who favored Jacob's twin over him (you might remember the story of Isaac loving Esau more than Jacob). His *inward* lie is he believes he is not worthy of love (of course). His *outward* lie is that he believes there can't be a God who is a loving father type because fathers suck. His greatest fear is that he'll be a terrible father and end up just like his father (which happens, of course). His core need is to have his father's love, but he never gets it (makes me think of Robin Williams's great performance in *Seize the Day*). And deep inside, what he really wants and needs is God's love, and *that* he does realize he has, in the end (of course).

## Of Course, Of Course

Now, no doubt you noticed I put "of course" after everything up there. Why would I do that? Don't I want to sound innovative and original? I'm giving away the fact that I wrote something *predictable*! Of course I did!

Now, maybe you're even more confused. But, think. We want themes that are universal, that people all over can relate to. There are no unique new themes that are universal to all. And human behavior is such that it behaves for the most part in a logical way. So, of course if Jacob feels hurt by his father and has father issues, he's not going to believe God loves him. And we all swear we will never turn out like our parents but . . .

It's *not* a cop-out to give your characters predictable motivational behavior. These things work and make sense *because* they're believable. If I had set Jacob up so that his core need and fears were in contradiction or unrelated to the lie he believes and the hurt he's suffered that has created his persona, I'm *not* going to have a believable character.

Does this make sense? If his core need is to get his father's approval, but his greatest fear is falling off high places, and the lie he believes is he's the smartest human ever born, he's going to come across as a lunatic in need of a nifty straightjacket. Which is fine if the theme of my novel revolves around insanity.

So don't randomly give your characters attitudes, behavior, and beliefs. Make sure everything they do, say, and feel is grounded in who they are and what life experiences they've had. Focus more on the internal qualities rather than the external, superficial ones.

In the next chapter we'll look into some other ideas using additional character-developing techniques I utilize in planning my novels.

Think about . . . spending some time mulling over your characters and these three essential components to their personalities. Spend more time thinking about their inner motivation instead of their outward attributes. Think of some hurt in their past that will serve the plot and premise of your story in the best way.

## Chapter 14: The Clash of Characters

*"I just love real characters. They're not pretentious, and every emotion is on the surface . . . their likes, their dislikes, their loves, their hates, their passions."*
~film director David O. Russell

We discussed how you can take an ordinary character and make him fascinating by developing those three essential components to his personality: his core need, his greatest fear, and the lie he tells himself based on the wound he received early in life. I showed how my character Jacob in my novel *Intended for Harm* was all about father issues, and that tied in with my main theme. I pretty much had that as a basic idea when I started planning. (You'll notice I usually use the word *planning* as opposed to *plotting*. It's not because I'm against plotting, but I want to de-emphasize that structuring and growing you novel is not all about plot. Plot is important, but a plot with no heart, as I've mentioned, is just a plot.)

But then I had eight other main characters (POV characters) to develop, as well as a small handful of secondary characters. Since my secondary characters only had some bit roles, albeit essential to the story, I didn't spend as much time going into these three main elements of their personalities. I still made them rich characters, and I suppose if I thought about it for a few minutes, I could easily come up with their needs, fears, and lies as well. I think I do this now so subconsciously with all my characters that it comes out as I write. However, I'm talking *minor* characters that pop up in a scene or two. But for all other characters that are integral to your story, you will want to spend time thinking about these things.

Jacob marries Leah while he's at college. She gets a little wild, and pushes him into marriage, then pops out four kids, one after the other (she suffers from postpartum depression and is only happy when pregnant). Eight years later, she runs off with a rock band and abandons her family. So, I had to create these four children, since I knew the reader was going to watch them grow up for the next thirty or so years. That put somewhat of a burden on me to get a good understanding of family dynamics. Jacob ends up with six kids (he has two more after he marries Rachel), and each of those kids needed to be not just different but *believable*.

## Have a Reason for Each Characteristic

Now, I could have come up with a nice diverse list of personality traits (maybe even grabbing some random characteristics from the Meyers-Briggs formula) and doled them out for variety, but I did not want to do that. Instead, I thought long about how Reuben, the firstborn, would have felt. What is the big hurt he experiences? When he's seven years old, his mother leaves him. He's the firstborn and oldest, so I gave him firstborn qualities. Firstborn children often feel they have to be grown-up. They can be serious and overly responsible. Maybe not always, but setting Reuben up to have those tendencies is believable. So what lie does he believe? That it's his fault his mother left (very typical), and if he had been a better son, she wouldn't have left.

Starting with this, I envisioned Reuben as a sweet child but a burden to his dad (Jacob did not want Leah to get pregnant), which is something he senses. I also decided, then, to make the next child, Simon, be Leah's favorite. That exacerbates Reuben's low sense of self-worth and the lie he believes. If he sees how much his mom loves Simon, he believes more deeply that he's a nothing. This then becomes a repeat of Jacob and his father—a son wishing to please his dad but feeling he's failed. Hence, I tied in with my overarching theme. Reuben's core need, of course, is to have his father love him, and by the time he's an adult, the two of them have worked through some of this and there's healing there. But I made it a rocky road the whole way.

Now, Simon has other issues. He's been the loved child of the bunch, so when his mom bolts when he's five, he's furious. I made him a hot-tempered, volatile personality. The lie he believes is that women are evil and traitorous. He's so hurt and angry, he goes through life distrusting women. When his father remarries, Simon wages war with Rachel, the new "mom," for years. His greatest need is to have his real mother's love again, so when he's eighteen and he seeks Leah out, you can only imagine what happens when his long-awaited dream explodes in his face.

## Now Watch Them Clash

Now, when I put Reuben and Simon together in scenes as they grow up together, you can see how their issues will underlie their interaction. You can picture the arguments as Reuben tries to dutifully be a better son to his new mother, whereas Simon tries to sabotage her inclusion in the family every way he can. Your characters will clash if their core needs, fears, and lies threaten one another.

Then I have four other children, four other intense sets of dynamics introduced. If you recall the Bible story, Joseph is Jacob's favorite, and because Joseph outwardly receives such favoritism, Jacob's brothers all hate him. By the time he graduates high school, they are after him with murderous intent and drug him and throw him off a freeway overpass hoping to kill him. Joseph is a bit arrogant and gifted, which makes showing him favoritism all the more easy for Jacob. Not only that, he's the love child between Jacob and his new wife, and it's expected that merged families will foment some conflict and resentment between integrated siblings. All these dynamics are typical, which helps make the motivation and actions of my characters not only believable but relatable.

I hope by sharing this process with you I'm giving you ideas on how to grow and nurture your characters into deep, compelling ones. You need to have your themes in mind, and then work from your protagonist outward. You want to think about having traits that are common or expected to some extent, like Reuben's firstborn issues. You don't have to have them, but they offer a great framework to work within. Again, think *universality.*

Think about . . . taking two or three of your characters that you've worked on developing (and now have those three components well entrenched) and look at the dynamics between them. How can you make their core needs clash? How can their lies trigger a reaction in the others?

## Chapter 15: Character Arcs

*"Any change, even a change for the better, is always accompanied by drawbacks and discomforts."*

~author Arnold Bennett

I've never quite understood the use of the word *arc* when talking about plot and character. I keep picturing a big boat in a very heavy rainstorm. But seriously, even the image of an arc (shaped like a rainbow—which brings us back to the other ark . . . hmm) confuses me. For if you are creating a character arc showing some sort of progression of a character's inner growth through your novel as a bow that goes up and then comes down, it feels to me as if the character didn't go anywhere. They end up on the same line or plane. So I have trouble using that term.

### A Journey, Not an Arc

However, I am concerned with character growth, and it's a big, essential part of your story to take your protagonist on a journey of the heart that starts in one place and ends up in another. Just as a literal journey can take us to new places where we see new things, so, too, a character taken on an inner journey should end up seeing new things about herself. (I have an easier time talking about this growth process in terms of journey instead of geometry terms; I wasn't all that great in math). So here's another thing I find helpful when creating characters and working out the growth they're going to experience by the end of the book.

## Persona to Essence

Remember how I discussed in previous chapters the way the character will start in his persona (the face he presents the world) and eventually discover and embrace his true essence? I've critiqued manuscripts in which the character has a set view of the world, and in one scene, because of a few things someone says to him, he completely changes and becomes a new man.

That's just not believable, people. Having your character change as events affect him happens *over time.* We all know how hard it is to change even one irritating habit. Our spouses have possibly been nagging us *for decades* about something annoying we do, and though we really mean to change, we find it so hard to do so. We are often dogmatic in our beliefs, and even passionate regarding the sports teams we cheer on—sometimes randomly chosen. But if someone tries to get us to switch loyalties . . . Enough said.

Once you have your basic plot all worked out, you can parallel it with your character's inner journey. This ties in with the MDQ we went over earlier, and, if you recall, your character has to not only arrive at his *plot* goal by the end of the book, he has to arrive at his *spiritual* goal as well, and that implies inner change—gradual change.

I use large charts and create something akin to a Gantt chart (a timeline, basically) for my plot. I often do so with my characters. In fact, for *Intended for Harm* I made a big chart with each character on a timeline with the vertical lines denoting years (I had to cover forty years) and the horizontal lines for the characters. This chart was specifically for the character journey, the spiritual MDQ process (yes, all your main characters should grow and change). Post-It notes work great on large charts since you can move them around, by the way. I make sure to keep them out of reach of my cats, who are great at dislodging the notes if I lay the charts flat on the table.

At the start of the timeline I have a note regarding the character's persona at the beginning of the story. At the end I have a note about where they'll be spiritually at the end—in their true essence, or at least indicating they're getting there. There's no rule that says your protagonist has to reach her goal.

Remember, the MDQ asks a question like "Will Indie Jones retrieve the Ark of the Covenant at the end of the movie?" (Hmm, another ark . . .) The answer might be no. Same with your character's spiritual goal. She may *not* come into her true essence by the end of the book. But unless you want a completely postmodern hopeless ending, you'll want to show some glimpse that she's on her way, which often is more believable than having her fully arrive by the last page.

## Change Comes in Stages

Once I have the first and last notes in place, I think of all the stages of change my character will go through. I might jot down a scene idea in a sentence stating something that happens to her or that she sees that will shift her view. Be sure to note how her view gets shifted. Remember, you have to change characters in *stages*, starting with their opinions and attitudes and eventually changing their core beliefs, which can sometimes take a lifetime (not for you to do this—I mean the character's lifetime, just to be clear here). Having an idea of concrete scenes that can facilitate or instigate these gradual changes will make your character's journey believable. Let me explain this in more detail.

## Build It Gradually

It's fine to have a character passionate about a belief or public policy or cause. And through that character you can showcase your theme. But you want to be careful that, in your desire to send a message to your readers, you don't sound like your pontificating or pushing your moral standards on your readers. You will just sound like you have an axe to grind, and that axe will end up falling on your own head by doing that. A compelling way to get your theme across is to have a character opposed at first to the belief you want them to eventually embrace, but this has to be done gradually and believably.

There is a great sequence of steps author James Scott Bell presents in a workshop showing the order in which a character has to change for it to be believable. These are the things that change in the character over time, in this order:

- Opinions
- Attitudes
- Values
- Core Beliefs
- Self-image

Long before a core belief in us changes, our opinions and attitudes must shift. Change comes in increments. Most people are gradually persuaded into a new belief system. Or not.

So, you can't have a character talking to someone about the death penalty (which he is all for) and just through that one conversation have his belief changed (fully against) right at the heart of his core belief. I bring this out because this is how you have to think of your theme as it grows through the novel. If you want to send a message that the death penalty is wrong, how better than to start with your protagonist who is all for it but through the journey of the story ends up convicted at heart completely opposed to it? Great novels and movies do this, and the changes their characters make are believable.

Okay, go ahead and call it an arc.

> Think about. . . your novel's plot. If you are far along or in the revision stage, this is a great time to draw a chart, write some sticky notes, and put them on the timeline in order. See where the holes are. You may need to either write or rework a scene so you can show a bit of change. Always keep in mind that you are moving toward your character going from persona to essence, but you do want some setbacks and backsliding. Usually close to the end your character will fall back into the person they were before because it's safe and they're ready to give up. You can put that on your chart too!

## Chapter 16: History as Mystery

*"What is past is prologue."*
~William Shakespeare

We've gone over some nifty things about character in the last few chapters. Hopefully by now you have gotten a great glimpse into how to create a complex, driven character. I'd like to add some more insights about character development now and get you to think about history as mystery.

I mentioned how it's not all that helpful (or interesting) to spend time creating the outward attributes of your character, for what really shapes a person is their history. I showed how by creating and exploring a character's past hurt or wound you can determine the way she looks at herself and the world. When your character believes lies about herself and her world because of this hurt, she creates a persona that's not her true self. And when someone is not her true self, she feels restless, unhappy, and lost. Which spurs her on a journey to find her essence. It's the place she needs to get to, and her journey through the novel is not just aimed at her reaching her visible plot goal but also her spiritual goal of embracing her essence or who she truly is. Remember the sixties and how we were all about "finding" ourselves? This is the same thing but without the drugs.

## Create Some History

So once you've established this pivotal element or incident (or series of incidents) that have made her who she is at the start of the story, you'll want to create some more history. With that major task out of the way, the next step is giving your characters an entire life. This doesn't mean you have to write or know every single second in their past. But you want to create enough of a past that they fill out. And the events and history you create need to be homogeneous with who they are now as well as fit in with your plot.

I really love Elizabeth George's book *Write Away*. She has a whole section showing how she freewrites about a character, and I think she's spot on (okay, she writes British mysteries so I had to say that). I take her writing advice seriously because she's one of my favorite authors and a terrific writer. And nobody, at least in my opinion, writes better characters.

She has a prompt sheet that she uses to do a workup on each main character. It lists things like core need (heard that one recently?), ambition in life, gestures when talking, age, best friend, strongest character trait, weakest trait, hobbies, what she does when alone, and other details both physical and internal. She also lists "significant event that molded the character" (which is a variation of my "wound caused that makes them believe a lie"). She also reprints a number of pages that she typed while freewriting about a protagonist in one of her novels. Which is what I'm suggesting you do (the freewriting, not the reprinting).

## Getting to Know You

Take some quiet time, just you and one of your characters, and get to know each other. Start writing about her. Let the words flow, and don't edit yourself or censor. Start talking about who she is, where she came from, what she thinks and cares about. Just ramble. As writers we know all about creative inspiration, and we experience it (hopefully often) while we write our scenes. Call it muse or divine inspiration, but freewriting, like journaling, can draw from a deep well of experience and emotion. Things float to the surface of the mind when you do this, and I will guarantee that some of your best ideas for your character will come through this exercise. You are delving into the mystery of your character, and this exercise will bring out their secrets.

One variation of this exercise is to write in first person and let the character talk to you, emote, rant, go off anywhere she likes. You may want to do this for an hour or a number of times over days. When I wrote *Intended for Harm* I decided I would give each character one full day of my attention, and so as I went through my day, not just while sitting and freewriting and ideating but also while making dinner and vacuuming the house, I conversed and meditated on my character and let him or her grow organically. I think that's a great word to use because I don't believe you can force a character to appear in all her fullness in a few minutes. Like a good stew, she needs time to simmer so the flavors can come out. (Okay, that's a weird simile, but, oh well.)

Interestingly (and what I love best about writing fiction!), at some point the characters become real to you. As your personality and needs and fears and passions start infiltrating into your characters, you start to care about them. If you are starting your novel and you don't care at all for all your main characters (including your antagonist), you haven't done enough homework. I can't stress how important this is. Doing or not doing this work might mean the difference between an okay novel and an amazing one. And who wants just an okay novel? Not me, no way.

## Reduce It Down

Of course you aren't going to use all the material in those fifty pages you wrote. Go through and highlight the best lines that work great in characterizing your character, and pick the bits of history that make her the unique person she is. You may only use a small bit in your novel, and maybe almost none of all that history you wrote. So why do it? Because knowing your character's history will show even if you don't write about it. Trust me, it's true.

You can tell when someone truly knows their character inside and out, even if they tell you almost nothing of their past. You need to know all that because it will shape how you write her in every scene—her speech, thoughts, movements, choices, etc. At some point you will feel you are ready to tell her story.

I always know when that moment is. And if I've done my work and planned out my novel (which involves those cool charts and index cards), I'm good to go. Do I ever get writer's block? Never. Really. I never have. And it's not because I'm so amazing, because I'm not. It's because by the time I'm ready to start, I am so bursting with story and theme and character that the story just spills out. I believe you can be the same if you do your prep work and resist beginning until the pieces are in place. Think about it for your next novel.

Think about . . . taking one character who you don't feel is very complex or deep and do some freewriting—either in first or third person. Let yourself write about not just what you already know about her but all kinds of other things from her past and what she feels. See if anything you write is good enough to merit a place in your novel.

## Chapter 17: Bad Guys Aren't All That Bad (or at least they shouldn't be)

*"Things were easier for the old novelists who saw people all of a piece. Speaking generally, their heroes were good through and through, their villains wholly bad."*

~W. Somerset Maugham

I want to take a little bit of time talking about bad guys. Most novels have an antagonist. Not all, but somewhere along in your novel writing career you will probably have one bad guy (or gal) show up. Writers really have a tendency to lean toward the stereotype with antagonists, and maybe that's because we're such nice people and don't really know any evil folks, and so we don't have a clear idea what a bad guy really is like . . . except from all those superhero movies we watch. And those are only adding to the problem of badly created antagonists in our novels.

Maybe some writers feel the antagonist doesn't have to be a sympathetic character. Why in the world (you may ask) would I want my reader to sympathize with that creep? Well, I'm going to give you a good reason, so hold that thought. As with any and every character in our novel, we want our bad guy to be believable. And what have we discussed about creating believable characters? That they are complex, contradictory, and they have a past that has made them who they are.

Past is key with your antagonist because usually there is something that happened way back when to your character that has made him (or her) into the vile, despicable person he is today (or at least on the day in your novel when he's introduced). And sometimes when we get an understanding of why a person behaves the way he does—what made him that way—we often can muster up some compassion for him. Face it—bad guys aren't always 100 percent bad, just as good guys aren't perfect. No one will relate to a hero/protagonist that has no flaws, and no one will believe an antagonist that has no redeeming qualities.

## Characters You Love to Hate

I'm a big *Star Trek* fan, and for those of you who have watched *Deep Space Nine,* you'll know what I'm talking about when I say the Cardassians are a great example in a collective way of the antagonist/bad guy that has contradictory qualities. Cardassians are very cruel and heartless, void of mercy, and yet they are extremely affectionate and tender toward their children and devoted to their wives. Gul Dukat is one of the best characters in the series due to his complexity and seeming contradictions. You can hate him all your want, but there are those moments . . .

## A Glimpse of Vulnerability Goes a Long Way

And this is where you'll want to do some special work on your antagonist. You are not risking anything by having your reader feel a little sympathy or empathy for him. *Ever After* is the great example of a movie that portrays the perfect antagonist. Anjelica Huston's character is such a horrible, wicked stepmother that you hate her guts. And yet the screenwriter did a fantastic job by writing the one and only scene (moment) in which we see a hint of her humanity and actually feel something for her. It's truly brilliant.

In that scene she tells Danielle [read: Cinderella] to come over and brush her hair. For just a moment she softens and mentions how the girl looks so much like her father (although she has to poison the line by commenting on how manly her features are). Danielle then asks her if she loved Auguste, her father, and the stepmother says sadly that she didn't really know him all that well. She shares a little insight into her childhood and the way her mother raised her, giving her a history we can imagine—and almost empathize with.

This is such a subtle but powerfully tender moment where for a second we see not just a soft side to the evil stepmother but a fragility and vulnerability. In that one moment we can understand why she is so scheming and ambitious and mean. We see her deepest fears in her face—maybe the fear of being alone, of losing everything. She still goes on to do hateful things, and in the end we are glad she gets her just desserts because she doesn't change right then—not at all. But by getting that moment of a glimpse into her soul and the hurt she holds inside, she becomes a much richer and more believable character. We understand her motivation and why she is so mean. We don't condone her behavior, but she is now fully real to us—even in a fairy tale structure such as this. Which is what makes *Ever After* one of the best fairy tales movies ever made.

## Flip the Script

Before you say you don't have a clear antagonist in your story, think about a character that opposes your protagonist. It could even be a good friend. In some instances, supportive characters take on the role of an antagonist, so try to broaden your perspective a bit as we go a little deeper into understanding your antagonist and working on making him more human (unless he isn't human, as might be the case in a sci-fi novel—but he still needs to have some agreeable "human" traits, so if you think you can get out of doing this because of the genre you're writing in, you have another *think* coming).

Ask: What is the worst trait of your antagonist? Is she heartless? Judgmental? Cruel? Take a moment and challenge your brain to come up with a moment and situation in which you could show a glimpse of *exactly the opposite*. Remember the example I just gave of the wicked stepmother in the movie *Ever After*, showing how the writer created a scene specifically to reveal a bit of vulnerability of that character. That scene could have been left out of the movie (in which she has a "heart-to-heart" talk with her stepdaughter in the bedroom) and the movie would still have been great. That scene was not at all crucial to the plot—not one bit. Yet, I feel that scene is one of the most important ones in the movie, and I'm sure you can guess why. I love seeing the flip side to the bad guy, getting a peek at his humanity. I guess I just want to believe everyone is redeemable deep down inside. And I think that's a belief that resonates inside a lot of us. But we can still hate the bad guy anyway.

## Bad Guys Have a Story to Tell

What does your antagonist want more than anything else? Can you think of showing a moment where she might waver in that desire and reconsider? Where she has a moment of hesitation about the evil she is perpetrating? Have second thoughts? This is where you could get a bit in about their greatest fear because often fear is at the core of why we do sucky things to other people. We lash out and hurt others to prevent ourselves from feeling hurt. And again, this goes back to the wound from the past. Just what happened to your antagonist way back when to make him so awful? Does he carry guilt over something shameful he did? Or something he should have done and didn't?

Once you come up with a good reason for your antagonist opposing your protagonist, you can create a moment where that memory of the past hurt is triggered. Maybe something happens in a scene that makes your bad guy remember what it felt like to have that done to him. Maybe he's about to beat up his kid and flashes back to when his father beat him and winces at the painful remembrance of that time. You don't want to give your antagonist a quickie unbelievable change of heart; you want to show a little of why he is the way he is to garner a little empathy.

Maybe you think this is a waste of time and counterproductive to your plot. After all—you want the reader to hate your bad guy, not feel for him. But I'd like to encourage you to try this and see if it doesn't make that antagonist more believable.

The movie *The Runaway Jury* comes to my mind. Isn't there a moment at the very end of the movie when Gene Hackman's character, the lawyer Fitch, is watching Nicholas and Marlee (the heroes) back in their hometown after he's learned the whole truth about who they are and why they rigged the jury? He seems to be almost sympathetic in his expression, as if he gets why they destroyed his career. He doesn't say anything, show any remorse—you wouldn't want that anyway. He's the bad guy, and we feel he got what he deserved. But I like to think at his moment of understanding you can tell there's a bit of humanity underneath him. His expression hints at admiration for what they did.

Of course, in your novel, you have to find another way to show this sensitivity, and it can be done through the eyes of another character (maybe your protagonist sees something in her antagonist's face), in the antagonist's thoughts or deep POV, or by some subtle action he may engage in that shows he has some feelings.

## Show a Little Compassion

A great exercise Donald Maass had us "breakout novelists" do at his workshop was to rewrite our synopsis from the POV of our antagonist. At first I thought that was a little weird, since I didn't write my original synopsis from my protagonist's POV—I wrote it from my POV, but I gave it a try. Wow, it was great! Suddenly a different tone took over. What happened was I began to see, as I outlined the plot and premise from my evil mother character's take, was a whole new side to the story. She looked at the whole situation and conflict with her daughter in an entirely different way and really believed that the cruel choices she was making were justified—they were for her daughter's own good, in her mind.

Writing this caused me to mentally step back again, and it made my antagonist so much more understandable. How can you truly hate someone who does horrible things to her family if deep in her heart she really believes she is doing the right, moral, and best thing for those (she thinks) she loves? From that, I was able to rework some scenes to give my "evil mother character" more sides, and I hope I made her at least a bit more believable and well rounded.

Think about . . . (if you have an antagonist in your book), taking a good look at him or her. See if this character is just a flat stereotype or is complex. Does this character have a redeeming quality? If you haven't shown it, find a place in your book to reveal this. It can be shown through dialog, action, or internalizing. Play around with this and see if you've made your antagonist better and more believable. If you are still in the planning stage, come up with a rich past ,as I've discussed in earlier chapters, then give your antagonist one vulnerable quality or moment that's not trite but genuinely shows a human side.

If you're game, try writing your synopsis in the POV of your antagonist. Or if you don't have one written or want to try something different, freewrite in her POV and let her explain the moral reasons for behaving the way she does. Let her talk about her past and how she became who she is. She may not think she's evil at all. Or she may feel her cruelty is quite justified. Then work some of this into your novel and see if your stereotyped character now looks a little more real.

# Chapter 18: Secondary Characters Have a Life of Their Own

*"If the smaller characters are well-written, the whole world of the film becomes enriched. It's not the size of the thing but the detail."*

~actor Brendan Gleeson

We all need a supporting cast in our novels. Secondary characters have to be in there, unless your book is about a guy stuck on a deserted island the entire time or in some other solitary circumstance. But even in that instance, an animal or even a volleyball (sorry, had to put that in there from *Castaway*) can play the role of a secondary character. There are plenty of great movies in which even the hero is an animal (*The Incredible Journey* is one that comes to mind) or something not human. But whether your secondary characters are human, feline, canine, or bovine, they need to be fully human in their characteristics (well, maybe cats can getting away with just saying no).

## They Stick in Your Mind

To be honest, I don't come across a whole lot of manuscripts that have many terrific secondary characters. And I struggle with creating good ones in my novels. The tendency is to throw someone in there only as a vehicle to bring out the plot or reveal aspects of the protagonist's personality, but when we do that, the reader can sense it.

I love a great book in which a secondary character almost steals the show. Right away I think of Fermin, the oddball street guy in Zafon's best seller *The Shadow of the Wind*. His performance throughout the book riveted me without taking away from the story in any way. Another character that has stuck with me for decades is Le Cagot, a Basque nationalist and lunatic in Trevanian's novel *Shibumi*. If you haven't read those terrific novels, I highly recommend them—if only to learn how to craft great supporting characters.

Think about Sherlock Holmes's sidekick Watson. My husband and I have watched just about every Sherlock Holmes movie and TV episode made in the past century (as well as read all the stories many times). We even went to 221 Baker Street when we were in London—just so we could feel what it was like to walk on that street. Watson is a real character in his own right, and although he can hardly overshadow such a larger-than-life character like Holmes, he does stand out as a well-rounded person because we see who he is *apart* from Holmes. He has a life when Holmes suddenly disappears from his apartment (which Holmes tends to do a lot).

## Tell Them to Get a Life

This is what you want to think about as you create and develop your secondary characters. They do not live for your protagonist; they all have lives that take place in their world when they are not in those scenes with your lead player. The more you can give them a life outside the novel's scenes, the better. Don't settle for giving them a past and some physical attributes. Spend some time thinking about what their life is now. Ask: What would this character be doing if I removed the protagonist from the story? What would his life look like? What problems would he be facing in his personal life right now?

Giving secondary characters a problem that is unconnected to the plot is a great element to add. Why? Because now you have a subplot. And don't just give them any problem; think of something that can tie in with your theme and enhance the main plot. This is what secondary characters can do best.

## Make Their Needs Clash

Here's an example. Let's say you are writing a novel about a woman named Debby who is struggling with infertility issues. Her goal is to get pregnant, and she's in despair trying everything to conceive. Her need is destroying her marriage and affecting her job performance. But she is so grateful for her best friend Joan. Joan isn't married and doesn't have kids, and she's been BFF (best friends forever) with Debby since kindergarten.

Now, Joan's got a boyfriend who is pushing the relationship, and she's not sure how committed she is. Whereas Debby's been married for some time and is committed, but her husband is pulling away (kind of the opposite). Just when things are really falling to pieces with Debby (who may not be letting on just how badly she wants to have a baby), Joan accidentally gets pregnant. She's in turmoil about this because she's not married and doesn't want a baby at this point. What does she do? She tries to tries to keep this news from Debby, knowing it might upset her. But Debby finds out—right when Joan has decided to have an abortion.

Now you have some great conflict. Their friendship will be stretched because these two characters' deepest fears and core needs are clashing. I can envision a lot of tears flying as Debby, shocked, tells Joan not to abort.

I've read a lot of books that have subplots thrown in that have little connection to the main plot. And those secondary characters involved in those subplots have a disconnect with the protagonist. What I'm trying to show here is that if you create secondary characters who have a life of their own, with their own needs and fears, *and* make those things clash with the protagonist's visible and/or spiritual goal (as discussed in earlier chapters), you will enrich your story a thousandfold. Don't leave them stranded outside, waving their hands and hoping you'll notice them. Bring them to the fore, and give them their time in the limelight.

Developing great secondary characters really helps get to the heart of your story. As I mentioned above, having those secondary characters' needs and fears clash with those of your protagonist will drive the plot toward the mother lode—the heart of your story. That's just one way you can not only bring your secondary characters to life but also enhance your overall theme. I'm big on themes, and I believe books with well-explored themes can have great impact on the reader.

So as you consider your secondary characters and create their lives and personalities, think of a problem they come to face as the book unfolds that will tie in with the theme.

## Create a Moment

Here are some other things to think about regarding secondary characters. It's good if you can come up with a moment or two in the novel that is a special highlight of the relationship between this character and your protagonist. Maybe this is a moment where one of them gets an insight about the other or changes how they feel for the other in some way (for good or bad).

When you think of various friends you've spent time with over the years, do any particular moments come to mind? What about that uncomfortable time where one of you did or said something unintentionally hurtful, and the fallout from that incident lasted a few weeks before getting resolved? What about the time when your friend revealed something shocking to you? I can remember the moment my good friend Bob confessed to me he had AIDS. He worried that I wouldn't want to be his friend anymore. I recall the wash of emotion that went through me as I sat there with him. That moment changed the dynamics of our relationship and took it to a deeper level—a level we enjoyed for a number of years until he died.

If you can create a specific moment in your novel where something special or intense or important passes between the protagonist and this secondary character, it will do wonders for your story. So many moving, poignant scenes in movies are ones in which the two friends have a moment like this. It feels sometimes like a beat or pause in the story, being more reflective and slower paced. But it adds heart, and that's what we're after as we journey through the mine to reach the mother lode.

Let that "minor" character show some depth of emotion, and not in reaction only to the plot playing out or to what the protagonist does. You don't want this to be a forced mushy moment—you may be writing a suspense/thriller. But even then, you could have that short pause in which your protagonist and work colleague have a talk. Let the protagonist learn something new about this other person, get some new insight about them. Let the secondary character see something new in the protagonist.

## They Don't Always Get Along

Think also about creating one moment in which this secondary character is really opposed to what the protagonist is saying or doing and voices this opinion. Allies in stories are sometimes called "refection" characters. That is, they reflect back to the protagonist things that he might not be able to see about himself—or like. That can cause conflict.

Also consider finding a moment in which you can switch this role and have the protagonist opposed to what the secondary character is saying or doing. When are they the most at odds with each other? Often it's when one or the other has made a big decision. It's often a turning point in the story, and it tests their friendship or work relationship. Most plots involve the protagonist going off on a course that stirs up conflict and opposition, so that's probably where you would have this moment. And this is another way you can tie in theme, as the secondary character can act as an antagonist, taking an opposing view and challenging the protagonist's beliefs and actions, helping bring your theme to the forefront.

Ask this: How is my protagonist *changed* by the end of the story by something this other character says or does? If you can set up a way for this secondary character to influence your protagonist in a way that helps or hinders her from reaching her visible goal, she will become an intrinsic and valuable member of your "cast."

Think about . . . taking a look at your secondary characters. Make sure you've created a life they live outside the novel's main plot. Think what their story would be in your novel if your protagonist went away on vacation for a year. What would they be doing? Bring some of this into the scenes with your character. Try to come up with a subplot that clashes with the protagonist's visible goal. This takes work, but your novel will be so much better for it!

Think also about creating some moments described above. Find a place in the novel where you could insert a pause with a significant moment between your protagonist and this other character. Think of one other secondary character with whom you can do this with as well but in a different situation and way.

This wraps up the section on characters. I hope you've been challenged and inspired to write not good but great characters, and you can see the importance of giving each character a rich history, as well as an assortment of needs, fears, dreams, and lies they believe. Characters are the heart of your story, and if you create unforgettable characters, your book will be an unforgettable one that people will talk about long after they've read it.

# Part Three: The Heart of Your Plot and Theme

## Chapter 19: The Plot Thickens

*"Essentially and most simply put, plot is what the characters do to deal with the situation they are in. It is a logical sequence of events that grow from an initial incident that alters the status quo of the characters."*
~Elizabeth George

Now that you've created and developed some terrific characters, we're going to take a brief look at theme and plot. You'll notice this book barely touches on plot. Why is that? Plot is of *huge importance* to reaching the heart of your story. In fact, if your book has a plot with no heart, it will flop out of the starting gate, and the supporting walls leading to the mother lode in your mine will collapse a few feet in. I'm a stickler for tight, engaging, and well-thought-out plots. Even though I consider myself a character-driven writer, I make no concessions—in my own novels or in those of my clients'—for any weakness or plot holes.

But because plot is such a rich topic and volumes can be written about it, I'm going to save all that for a future book—for I have way too much material about plot to include in this one instructional book. Suffice it to say, there are some terrific books at your disposal that are all about plot, and so I would encourage you to pick up a few—especially James Scott Bell's *Plot and Structure.* And there is a ton of information on the web about plots and how to write them. I certainly don't want to repeat all the great material you can find out there. So I'm not going to go into the basics on how to structure a plot. This book is all about looking at the heart of your story, and so my focus is more on *why* you're writing the story you are and what passion you are bringing to it.

I would, though, like to share some thoughts I have about layering plots, since this ties in so nicely with what we looked at regarding secondary characters and the need for them to have their own lives and subplots.

## Plots—Bigger Is Better

I'm going to assume for now you have your plot all worked out. Maybe you've already written your novel and you're in a revision stage. Maybe you're at the place where you think your plot is pretty darn good and doesn't need any work, and you're focusing more on enriching your characters or subplots. Wherever you are with your novel, I'd love to offer some thoughts and suggestions on ways you can look deeper at your plot and maybe push the edges a bit to make it bigger.

Sure, you can add some more subplots, and if those are done well, they will add a lot to your story in terms of revealing character and emphasizing your theme (which we are just about to look at). But your main plot is your story, and there's a reason you wrote it.

## Ask and Ye Shall Make It Worse

If you haven't done this at all at any time before or during the writing of your novel, I'd like you to consider spending some quiet time asking yourself these questions after identifying your theme and the take-away thought or message you want to give your readers when they finish reading your book. Your protagonist has a goal and is facing a problem to get there. Ask:

- What's the problem about? How can I make it bigger? If I take my protagonist out of the story, what does that problem look like in universal terms?

- How can I make this problem the protagonist has harder? How can I make things worse in the outer world and in his personal life?

- How can I make the effects of this problem worse for other people as well? How can I broaden the scope of this problem so it affects a greater scope?

- What does this problem push people to do that they wouldn't normally do? How can I blow that up bigger and make them do worse things?

- How can I make it harder for my protagonist to solve this problem? How can I raise the stakes so more is at risk? If I have just one thing at risk, what other things can I add and put at risk?

These are just a few questions to get you revisiting your plot from a distance. You may feel locked in with your protagonist going through certain doors and overcoming a set number of obstacles to reach the end. But if you can make your story bigger and more complex in some ways, you will have a plot that is richer and works on many levels. For example, if you have a man leaving his wife, his actions are affecting his wife and children. But what if his actions cause a snowball effect and by leaving he creates other problems? Maybe his wife is already on the brink of a breakdown, and this pushes her to do something terrible—like drive drunk and smash the car, which maims his child? What if leaving his wife creates repercussions at his job, causes him to make a deadly mistake that harms others?

### Make a Mess

You can freewrite ideas on paper. Just let them come. Think of more ways to make a mess for your protagonist. Even if you've already written the book, you can add layers by making the problem bigger, giving it a wider scope. You can have more people in the protagonist's world rocked by how he is handling his problem, which only makes it worse for him.

## Layers and Layers of Plot, Oh My!

Novelists do focus heavily on plot, and rightly they should. Your novel needs a well-crafted and believable plot. A good story will have one. A great story will have many plot layers. You could call them subplots, but I find it helps to think of them as layers because of the way they work in your story. Plot layers come in all thicknesses of importance, and if they are designed carefully, they will make your story a rich "cake" with unique and lasting flavors that will linger long after your reader finishes your book.

One way that may help you in developing and deepening your plot layers is to think about your own life. You have some big goals—long-term, long-range goals, or maybe even only one—on the horizon at the moment. Maybe it's to finish college and get that degree. Maybe it's to start a family and create your dream life with your spouse. In a novel, that might be your main plot, which features the visible goal your protagonist is trying to reach. This is the overarching plot that all the other plot layers will sit under. But just as with a multilayer cake, when you take that bite, the different flavors of the layers should complement each other and create a delightful overall taste.

## Life as Layers

As that "plot" plays out in your life, other things encroach or dovetail that goal. You may be dealing with some personal issue—like a recurring health problem or a former boyfriend who keeps showing up against your wishes. You may also be dealing with trivial issues, like trying to decide what color to paint your bedroom, and the paint store guy, who's completely incompetent, can't get the color right.

Life is made up of layers. I picture them by their size and scope. You have the big, fat layer of the main plot on top, then different layers underneath of different thicknesses and flavors. All this creates a very rich cake. If life were just one sole "plot" ("I gotta get that college degree"), it would be boring and so would you. And so are novels that only have one plot layer. Life is complex. It's messy. We're told to complicate our characters' lives. Well, this is the best way to do it—by introducing many layers of plot, and not just for your protagonist but for your secondary characters as well.

## Vary the Intensity of Each Layer

If you can create three layers at least, think of them as plots A, B, and C. You know your A plot—it's the main one driving your story. But now you need B and C. You want B to be an important layer that will help the main plot along—either something that enhances Plot A or runs headlong into conflict with it. Plot C will be thinner and more trivial, and may even add that comic relief in your tension (picture your character trying to get the paint guy with myopia to see the obvious difference between the two unmatching paint swatches).

Take this a step further and imagine one of your secondary, supportive characters in your novel dealing with an issue that juxtaposes with your protagonist's issues. Remember the example of Debby, who was fighting infertility, and at her peak of despair at being unable to conceive, her best friend Joan not only learned she'd accidentally gotten pregnant—she'd decided to get an abortion. Can you see how this plot layer can add depth to your story by providing a place to reveal more of your protagonist's needs, fears, and personality?

A mystery I wrote—*A Thin Film of Lies*—needed a big revision, so I decided to make a secondary character my protagonist. Fran is a bit sketchy in the original story; you know a little about her life, personality, and tastes. She's a homicide detective investigating the hit-and-run that frames my story. But now I needed to bring her to the forefront.

Not only did I deepen her involvement with the main plot and increase the number of her scenes, I added an ongoing, growing tension with her teenage son that exposed issues of trust and believability—elements that are primary themes of my main plot. Fran doesn't really believe in her perp's claims of innocence regarding the hit-and-run, nor does she believe her son's when he insists he didn't hack the school's computer. In the midst of all this, she hates the LA heat, which exacerbates her terrible asthma, so my Plot C is the aggravating element of her air conditioner at home always going on the fritz—which compounds the tension and "heat" in her house and family life.

And let me tell you a little secret that makes a ton of sense to me: Plot C is often a great catalyst to revealing important aspects of your character and story. Remember, it's often the little incidents in life that send us over the edge or trigger a breakdown or breakthrough.

Ever fall apart when you can't get your car to start? What if you put your character at the edge of desperation and she needs to get somewhere fast—and then her car (the one she's been taking back and forth to the shop the whole novel) finally dies. Think of all the ways a Plot C can really mess things up. Usually the scenes dealing with Plot C are the pivotal ones in my novels.

Play with your themes. Brainstorm these plot layers, and then find places in your novel, or create new scenes, where you can add these in. If you do, you will end up with a delicious, irresistible story readers will love to dig into and that will lead to the heart of your story.

Think about . . . creating a list of ideas of how you can make the protagonist's problem bigger. Don't edit yourself as the ideas come. Let even the most ridiculous ideas end up on the page. Then, when done, see if you can find a few you can add to your plot to make it bigger.

Take a look at your plot, and if you don't have any B or C layers, think of one of each that will complement your main plot. Find places in which to bring these out, or create some new scenes to play out the new plot layers. You'll be amazed at how doing this will deepen the heart of your story.

## Chapter 20: Themes That Speak to the Heart

*"You can't tell any kind of a story without having some kind of a theme, something to say between the lines."*
~director Robert Wise

Time to dive into another big novel element that speaks directly to the heart of your story. I'm going to delve deeply into themes because I feel a great book always has a great (or more than one great) theme. Think about what Donald Maass writes in *Writing the Breakout Novel*: "Most authors launch into their manuscripts without giving any thought to theme. Breakout novelists, on the other hand, generally are writing for a reason. They have something to say. . . . When [readers] run across a novel that has nothing to say, they snap it closed and slap it down—or perhaps hurl it across the room."

Wow, that's a pretty strong statement, but coming from a top literary agent, we have to assume he knows of what he speaks. He brings up something that's interesting to me: "Why do opinionated people bother with novels, which have challenging things to say? Novels are moral. . . . For the most part they validate our values. And no matter what your values, there are novels to affirm them. . . . Readers tend to seek out the novels that accord with their beliefs. They want their values validated, true, but usually not in a simplistic, moralizing way. They may not want to be converted, but they do want to be stretched."

## We Are All Opinionated

I agree with Maass that although we may have opinions about things, as writers we need to be passionate about things. I mean, think about it. Why in the world would you spend a big chunk of your life writing a novel if you don't have anything significant or of value to say in it? Sure, it may just be a hilarious comic farce meant to entertain, but with a theme, it could become so much more. And a novel in any genre can benefit from theme.

Part of being a courageous, impassioned author is to be willing to share your passion through your writing. This doesn't mean you aim to write a book that sermonizes and hits readers over the head with your beliefs. It does mean, though, that you infuse some of this into your story by way of your characters. If you haven't spent any time thinking about a theme for your story, you may want to sit back and think.

## Yes, You Do Need a Theme

Do you really have to have a theme for your book? Not necessarily in a formal sense, but think about theme as some essential take-away thought you want to leave your reader with when they finish the book. Theme speaks to your plot, but more so to the heart of your story. One way to get to your theme is to ask yourself why you are writing this book, anyway. Do you have a message or something you want to say to your readers, some commentary on life, society, government, faith, or some other issue? Even if you are not trying to push a "message" per se, your book should be about *something.*

If you think hard and can't come up with anything even barely important, meaningful, or significant about the story you want to tell, maybe you shouldn't be spending all these months writing this novel. Maybe that sounds harsh, but if you're not moved in some way by *something*

in your story, then why are you bothering to write it?

If you're just writing a page-turning thriller or a straight genre mystery or suspense, you might not need an overarching theme. You might still write an exciting book that entertains. But this book isn't aimed at writers seeking to pump out genre mass-market books without heart. It's not for writers just writing to make a living and that's it. This book is for writers who really have something to say, and that's exactly what we're dealing with right now—honing and paring down what you want to say in a phrase or two.

## Say It in One Sentence

If you were asked to tell someone in one sentence *why* you wrote your novel, what would you say? Can you think of something to say that will make the listener nod and say, "Wow, that's interesting (or needed or pertinent or important or . . .)" If you can't think of a significant take-away statement, then you might need to stop writing and start thinking. Because a book without a theme is like a day without sunshine. (How does that saying go? I think it's from a commercial about orange juice . . .)

Your theme or point—what the reader is getting into and why she should care—needs to be hinted at in the first page or two. A tall order? You bet. But if you can determine clearly why you're writing this story and what is the one thought, message, idea, conclusion, or feeling you want your readers to "take home" with them when they finish reading your book, you should be able to give some indication of this through your protagonist—by action, thought, or dialog—in those first paragraphs. Whatever that is must be set up in the first few pages, even if only a hint of a promise of what to expect. If your book is about forgiveness, then something about forgiveness or the lack thereof must be an important element of your opening scene.

I'm of the belief that your first scene should have at least something that hints at your theme. I feel the great books "out there" that have stood the test of time do this in some way. Bringing a hint of your theme out right away also clues the reader into what the book is *really* about, and reveals a bit of the heart of your story, which is what I'm all about.

Thinking about theme, I recall one exercise Donald Maass had us do in his week-long Breakout Novel Workshop. We were asked to write a brief summary of each of our book's scenes on index cards. Then we were to write the point of that scene on the back. He then told us to pull out the three cards that we felt contained the most important scenes in the book. I was surprised at which scenes I chose. And what was even more surprising (at least until I saw where he was going with this) was that all three scenes were similar and had the same component, i.e., theme. It pounded home the awareness of what my book was really about, and up until then I had some other ideas. What this showed me were the elements *I felt passionate about.* I didn't choose the best written scenes or the most tense or exciting. I chose the ones that moved me the most. And they were all scenes with moments of forgiveness.

## Pass the Popcorn

In the next few pages, I want to explore theme with you, and one easy way is to look at some of my all-time favorite movies. They might not be yours, and now that I think of it, most of them are considered light and funny. But their themes are so rich and deep that I'm thinking maybe they were such huge hits because of their underlying themes (that viewers didn't realize were there). In fact, I'm sure that's the reason. Because some of the acting in these movies is pretty awful—like hilariously awful (although I think it's true only with *Strictly Ballroom*, and that dialog is meant to be ridiculous). However, the scripts are brilliant. Okay, I'll throw *The Three Amigos* in there too, since I'm going to touch on that flick a little.

My recommendation to writers is this: search deep in your heart, if you want to tell a powerful story, and find the themes that resonate. Don't tell a story that means nothing to you—the reader will sense it and it will mean nothing to her. In a movie I saw years ago (I seem to recall it was *Rich and Famous*) the lead character says, "If your writing doesn't keep you up nights, it won't keep anyone else up, either." That line has stuck with me for decades in my writing journey. The more heart you put into your story, the more you will touch hearts. The more wrenched yours is as you write, the more likely you will wrench some of your readers' hearts.

## Finding Themes in a Brainstorm

Some writing teachers believe theme is either intrinsic in your story or it's not, but I disagree. Theme is a deliberate element, and it can be the core of your story. And as I've said before (and will give you my soapbox spiel at the end of the book), you really need to plan these things out in advance. Don't just jump into writing a novel when you get a cool plot idea or premise. Think for a while about the themes you may want to bring out that work in that story. After all, there has to be some reason you are writing it, and hopefully that reason comes from something in your heart. So bring it out.

## Brainstorm for Inspiration

You can always come back into a novel you've already fashioned and develop the theme, adding little bits of thought and dialog along the way. But if you're in the planning stage, all the better, for you can lay out your scenes with your theme in mind. I thought my novel, *Conundrum,* would be about betrayal, for I planned it to be gruelingly filled with lies and treachery. But the moment I sat down to brainstorm the theme, I filled a whole page with this rambling instead:

"Truth and lies. Searching for truth: it might not be found—is that okay? Truths differ from person to person. The *need* for truth differs from person to person. Sometimes it's better NOT to search for truth—who gets hurt in the process? What if you can't tell the truth from lies—does it matter? To whom? Do you have to get to the truth to find peace—or is there something more important? Does confessing truth bring more liberation than finding it? Is a search for truth worth the effort and fallout? If you are truthful to yourself, does it matter if everyone you love lies? Or that your life is founded on a lie?"

What happened, then, was the themes that emerged that really spoke to my heart ended up being the true heart of my story.

## Tapping into Your Passion

Where'd all that stuff about truth and lies come from? I really thought the theme of my book was something else. But when I let my passion infuse my planning, I came up with the bigger themes for the book. There are actually a few themes at work in *Conundrum*, as is the case with most of my novels; I like to complicate and enrich my stories as much as possible. I find exploring theme, when laying out a book, opens magical doors. Your subconscious comes to the forefront and may surprise you, as it did me. Theme seeps into character and plot, and twists motives. Sure, there will be subthemes that play along, but when you know your theme and you feel its truth validated in your heart as you begin your story, you have your foundation.

I was reminded of Vida Winter as I plotted *Conundrum*, the old author character in *The Thirteenth Tale*. She had told lies her whole life, but needed to tell the truth before she died. It was her greatest feat of accomplishment—getting deep and honest with herself, a place that terrified her. Another book with a theme about truth and lies. A beautiful book.

Think about . . . watching a great movie and considering the theme. It may not be obvious, but once you figure it out, it will glare at you like a blinking neon sign. Make a list of five of your favorite novels, then take some time to consider their themes. See if you can identify more than one for each novel. Usually great stories have multiple themes, and although these lesser themes may not be so obvious or as essential to the story as the main theme, they add richness to the story overall.

Think about the opening scene of a few of your favorite novels. Pick novels that you recall having a great opening scene. But this time as you read through the pages, pay particular attention to the hint of theme, the take-away message being set up early on. Great books showcase their theme from the start, however subtle. And it can be subtle, for sometimes you almost miss the implication of what's to come—a hint of the heart of the story coming through that will become full-blown by the end of the book. Some books that come to mind right away to me are *The Prince of Tides* (Pat Conroy), *My Sister's Keeper* (Jodi Picoult), and *Peace like a River* (Leif Enger). Can you think of some novels you've read that convey the theme in the opening scene?

## Chapter 21: Going to the Movies to Mine Themes

*"I hold any writer sufficiently justified who is himself in love with his theme."*
~Henry James

Okay, got your popcorn? I chose to look at movies for themes instead of novels. Why? Shouldn't we be looking at how novels convey theme? Yes, and it behooves writers to read a lot of well-written novels and explore how theme is developed in each one. However, more people have seen more of the same movies than they have read the same novels. And if you want to take a close look at how these themes have been brought out in the stories we're going to look it, it takes far less time to rent and watch a movie than it does to read a complete novel. Movies are no better or worse overall at showcasing theme, but one benefit to using movies as examples is that we all see the same exact thing on the screen, which makes it easy to discuss and visualize.

We're first going to look at the movie *K-Pax*—one of my favorites. Why do I love this movie so much? Because aside from the fact it tells a great story with heart and has a terrific and creative plot, it has very rich themes that anchor this movie and make it so very special. Although the story seems to be about some guy who claims to come from a faraway planet, it is not a sci-fi flick (as is the case with *Signs*, which also is really not about aliens at all).

## No, It's Not about Aliens

If you haven't seen *K-Pax* at least five times, you are really missing something. It is the consummate story of freedom from fear in all its aspects. Prot, from K-Pax, is truly messianic in the way he leads others to healing—not by a miraculous touch, though, but by showing each one their fear and the reality that they don't need to be afraid. Howie, Ernie, Bess—all the characters on the nut ward—are terrified of something: of dying, of dirt, of smells, of being touched.
And Prot gets them to understand why they are afraid and why they don't need to be. The healing and wholeness follows.

In one scene, Prot is explaining to the psychiatrist, Dr. Mark Powell, about his home world and how they don't need jails and punishment, or laws to regulate behavior. Powell asks, "Well then, how does one know what is right and wrong on K-Pax?" Prot makes a face of disbelief, then gives an astute answer: "Every being in the universe knows what's right and wrong, Dr. Powell." Powell replies: "What? No crime, brutality, no violence on K-Pax?" Prot answers, shaking his head sadly, "You humans. Sometimes it's hard to imagine how you've made it this far."

## It's Not about Prot Either

What's the theme in *K-Pax*? It's not about whether Prot comes from another planet or not—that's just the background of the real story. The protagonist of this film is Dr. Mark Powell, and his problem is his disconnect to his family. Throughout the movie, we witness the dynamics of his family—his alienation from his son, his distance from his wife, even his disconnect from his "family" of patients. As he uncovers the truth about Prot and the story behind Robert Porter and the horrific loss of family Porter underwent, we watch Mark come to the shocking realization that family is more precious than anything. He knows that Prot chose him, and wonders why. But we, the audience, know exactly why. He has an important life lesson to learn.

Dr. Powell undergoes a tremendous transformation, and we cheer him on. Of course, there are other beautiful themes in the movie. My heart aches thinking about Bess and how Prot notices
this invisible woman in the nut ward. There is so much messianic theme in this movie in metaphor. Prot tells Ernie to watch for the bluebird of happiness—that is his task—which Dr. Powell scoffs at.

Yet, the actual physical bluebird shows up outside the window. To Howie, this is all he needs. It may only be a bird to Dr. Powell, but to Howie it is a confirmation of his faith and a gift to his integrity. Big themes.

## Themes That Recur throughout the Story

Despite the variety of genre, style, writing, and tone, these movies I've picked to look at have a recurring universal theme that drives and weaves through the story. Authors can learn a lot from movies, but it's important to look beyond the spoken word—the dialog presented—to see what's really going on. And that's what happens in a great book. The universal themes waver just below the surface, occasionally rearing their heads when a character voices a question or makes a choice.

Admittedly, *The Three Amigos* falls short when it comes to building and weaving a theme, as the "El Guapo" speech given by Steve Martin at the end of the movie really serves as a rallying cry to embrace a theme in a last moment's spark of inspiration. But it deserves mention. How can you easily forget his brilliant words?

"In a way, all of us have an El Guapo to face someday. For some, shyness might be their El Guapo. For others, a lack of education might be their El Guapo. For us . . . El Guapo is a big dangerous guy who wants to kill us. But as sure as my name is Lucky Day, the people of Santa Poco can conquer their own personal El Guapo . . . who also happens to be the actual El Guapo."

You could get expansive and talk about how, throughout the movie, the three amigos really did have to face their "various" El Guapos—literal and emotional, since they lost their nice gig at the Hollywood studio. Hey, they did get to make off with their dazzling costumes. But enough of our friendly amigos.

## Another Movie Rich in Theme: *Strictly Ballroom*

I can't resist talking about my favorite movie—well, my entire family's favorite movie. We have to get our fix, watching *Strictly Ballroom*, nearly every time we're all home for a weekend. Although we can mouth and act out every line (can't quite master all the dance steps yet!), we never tire of this movie. We sit, absolutely transfixed, as we watch Francesca and Scott dance the Paso Doble. There are a few movies that hold the same fascination for me—and they all have one thing in common—great themes.

I often ponder why *Strictly Ballroom* holds so much sway over our hearts and attention. Why can't we get enough of this movie, even after having seen it dozens of times? *Back to the Future* is like that too. If I walk by the TV and it's on, it drags me over and forces me to sit down, and I'm mesmerized by every word. It's not just fun entertainment and snappy dialog. *Strictly Ballroom* has the same effect on me. It's rife with theme. Sure, it's a fairy tale—the ugly duckling makes off with the handsome prince, despite all odds. But it's so much more than that.

### A Theme That Is Presented by the Characters Themselves

Francesca, in a fit of frustration, mouths off a string of Spanish words, leaving Scott Hastings befuddled. She wants to dance with him in the Pan-Pacific competition, breaking the rules and dancing their own original steps, which is blatantly sacrilegious in the world of professional ballroom dancing. She translates the phrase: "A life lived in fear is a life half-lived."

It is no accident she utters this phrase. This "truth" is at the heart of every scene in this movie. This theme becomes Scott's awakening, his challenge, and ultimately his victory. It is the nectar the two drink, and the hope they embrace. It is the magical phrase that frees Scott's father from his "prison" and mends his parents' long-damaged relationship.

Nearly every character in this movie experiences both what it's like to live a life in fear and how empowered they are when they take a stand and face down that fear—which many do at the climax of the movie. This movie's brilliance is perhaps lost under all the makeup, costumes, and the histrionics of Shirley Hastings, but it's more than just the riveting music played during the Latin dance final that makes you want to jump to your feet and stomp your way around the living room. Your heart is soaring because the movie's theme successfully reached its target. By the end of the movie, you swear you will never live a half-lived life. You will not live in fear. Those are powerful themes conveyed in a comedic story—which should tell you that every genre can benefit from theme.

## The Deep Themes in the Movie *Nell*

Here's an amazing movie. Brilliant on so many levels. The plot itself is wonderful and enough to drive the story. But we see again another story in which there is a theme underlying the plot. *Nell* is not just about a girl who has spent most of her life in isolation. In *Nell*, we are put face-to-face with the question about our place in the world—what is considered normal and sane in the way we live our lives.

Two forces fight over Nell—those who want to let her keep her freedom, intent on proving that she cannot just survive but thrive without society. And the others, those in "authority," who insist Nell cannot care for herself, that she has to have others tell her what to think, eat, and wear; how to act; and how to live in a way that is not only acceptable but healthy.

If you haven't seen the movie, Nell is a young woman raised in the back country, who had never encountered or interacted with any people other than her family (don't want to do a spoiler here). A delivery boy discovers her right after her mother has died, and that tragedy has left Nell bereaved and alone. A doctor is asked to go talk with her, and thus begins the story of how Jerry, and then Paula, live on the property and study Nell, trying to communicate with her and assess her mental and emotional state. Does Nell need to be put in a state home? Or can she live on her own? Who has the right to decide?

## Small Things Are Big—and Not Just in Nell

Nell threatens the established norms, and as Jerry and Paula take her to court to try to protect her rights, in despair over her fate, Nell actually speaks up—in her strange manner of talking (because her mother, who had a stroke that impaired her speech, raised her with a warped version of English). To everyone's shock, Nell presents herself, with the help of Jerry's translating, as an intelligent, intuitive person. But most importantly, she understands the heart of life—what scares us, what moves us.

Nell tells us that she knows small things—her world is small. And that her listeners know big things, there in the city, in the big world. Yet, she sees how no one will look each other in the eye. She sees everyone's hunger for connection, for love, and asks why their world hasn't given them hope, love, or answers. She tells them she knows what it's like to love and to lose those she loves. She makes it clear she is no different from anyone else. But she can accept that those things are part and parcel of life. If that scene doesn't move you to tears, I would be shocked.

In this beautiful, haunting speech, she reveals she knows far more than most of her listeners. She has a wisdom that comes from reflection and true living. She doesn't just live in her world, she embodies it. She puts her opposers to shame with her honesty and compassion—something starkly lacking in those seeking to constrain her "for her own good."

One of the minor characters, a deputy, has a troubled, depressed wife. He is racked with despair, unable to find a way to help her, to show her how to find joy and peace in her life. Yet, when this woman meets Nell, she finds the help she seeks. Just watching Nell, talking to her, and being comforted by this young woman is the cure the deputy's wife needs. And there's a poignant moment in the movie in which this woman looks at Paula, the state psychologist sent to assess Nell, and she says, "You were the first one to need her."

Nell brings out many things in the people around her. They think they're there to help her, but the opposite is true. They each need to learn something about their fears and hang-ups, and Nell mirrors them innocently back to them. Everyone who gets around Nell is changed, just by virtue of her genuineness.

## Deep Themes below the Drama

So, what theme is going on here? I see it as this: Nell is considered helpless and unfit. Society is needed to tell us how to live and function, and we must be a compliant participant in order to not just survive, but to enjoy life. Life has rules and we're meant to follow them. Rules=happiness. The theme is that these are falsehoods. That sanity, happiness, functionality have nothing to do with society but have to do with your heart. That you can throw out every rule that doesn't speak to your heart because, in the end, those rules will not serve you or anyone else. That you have to face your fear and your pain to get to the raw truth of who you are. And that's too scary for most people, yet Nell, of all people, is there. She embraces her pain and loss in a beautiful acknowledgment that this is life—in all its beauty and despair. She challenges each one of us—can we live so honestly? How's that for a *big* theme?

Think about . . . watching one or all of these movies. If you have seen them before, try to watch them with new sight. Pay attention to the themes as they come out, and see how they are presented in the dialog and actions of the characters.

Think about the movies you love and why they touch you. Pick one, and see if you can find a universal theme that has been silently guiding the movie along. Then see how you can uncover the themes of what you are writing, and find ways to thread them through your story. You just might make someone jump out of their chair and dance around the room!

# Chapter 22: Lessons from a Pig and Some Guys Going through Midlife Crisis

*"The whole visible universe is but a storehouse of images and signs to which the imagination will give a relative place and value."*
~poet Charles Baudelaire

Before I start talking about a cool pig and the themes inherent in *Babe*, I want to add a little aside about symbols. Tying symbols in with a theme is very powerful, and the movie *Babe* does a great job with the gate as a symbol throughout the movie. I imagine few people ever really notice the bit about the gate other than the way it adds a bit of plot and humor, but it serves as another theme by way of symbolism.

## Symbols as Theme

Symbols are generally a visual object, but they can also be a thought, idea, phrase, or gesture. These can also be considered as motifs (chapter to follow), which are a terrific way to enrich your story and touch the reader's heart. But the great thing about symbols is they pack a lot of meaning in a simple way. When you use a symbol as a thematic element, you want it to reappear numerous times throughout your novel. *Babe* is a wonderful movie that wraps around a symbol.

## Come On-—Who Cares about a Pig?

Who would have thought such a simple, short children's book would have become such a blockbuster movie? A lot of children's movies are entertaining and funny for all ages, but *Babe* excels in a number of ways—not just in the quality of the animation and acting but because there are some great themes going on here. The most obvious one has to do with one's "purpose" in life.

Babe, spared by fate, finds himself confused and alone at Farmer Hoggett's farm. But he soon learns that every animal on the farm has a purpose—and so he goes about trying to discover what his might be. The theme is woven throughout the many characters—Rex the dog is in charge and has a noble purpose, but he feels ashamed that, because of a tragic occurrence, he cannot fulfill his purpose as well as he used to. The duck, on the other hand, is desperately seeking purpose, because—as the mean old cat cruelly informs Babe—those without a purpose end up like Roxanne: a duck cooked and steaming hot on the Thanksgiving table. But by the time Babe learns he has "a purpose," he has already demonstrated to Farmer Hoggett his wonderful "sheepdoggie" skills.

## Mind the Gate

Babe experiences a saving twist of fate, for Farmer Hoggett is a keen believer in divine purpose. His character is concerned with everything having a place, everything functioning efficiently. The symbol that ties in with this theme of purpose is "the gate." Using this subtle but powerful element, the writer of this script keeps us coming back to Hoggett tweaking his gate. Hoggett's aim is to have the gate close with a gentle touch and lock with the least amount of extra effort.

Likewise, he wants his farm to run smoothly, and part of that involves his dogs herding the sheep into their pens for various reasons. When he sees how Babe has acquired a knack for herding these sheep effortlessly, his attention rivets on the humble swine. Here is a pig with a destiny—with a purpose. Perhaps it is an unusual one, a strange and aberrant one. But Hoggett is not one to give a hoot what anyone else thinks—even when hundreds of people are laughing at him as he strides out into the arena with Babe as his "sheepherding dog" to compete in the time trials. He doesn't enter Babe so he can get attention or laughs, or to become famous or notorious. He enters Babe because it makes perfect sense. Babe is an excellent sheep dog, despite his porcine nature, and it is only logical for him to compete and earn the recognition deserved for his skills.

Hoggett is a man of few words, but we do get a sense of the affection he has developed for Babe when the pig appears sick and won't eat. Hoggett lapses into a sweet song and dance to cheer Babe up, which is exactly what Babe needs to fight off his depression and meet his destiny snout-on. Hoggett and Babe bond in purpose, and there is nothing so powerful as two linked together in such a manner.

By the end of the movie, Hoggett's gate closes perfectly, and Babe ends his sheepdog trial—to the astonishment of the flabbergasted audience—with Hoggett only making one simple move: lifting his hand to close the gate behind the sheep Babe has properly herded into the pen. That action with the gate is emphasized in slow motion and as a close-up—just so you will pay attention to the importance of the moment . . . and the symbol.

### No, It's Not Just about a Pig!

The audience in the stands jumps to their feet and cheers—and those watching the movie feel the same exhilaration. Babe and Hoggett have faced all odds and humiliating jeers and the weight of others' disbelief in them. But they shine victoriously because they proved faithful to their calling. They found their purpose in life and grabbed it by both hands (or trotters), despite every possible obstacle and discouragement.

This theme is huge when you realize the movie is not about a pig that just happens to have some special skills—that's not the theme at all. Because *Babe* explores a universal theme that each one of us struggles with daily—how to find our purpose in life and fulfill it—this movie met with enormous success. Take it from *Babe*—once you realize there are two kinds of stories—stories "with a purpose" and stories "without a purpose"—you will understand what you need to make your novel a breakout success. Learn this lesson from *Babe*—in your own life and in your writing—and look for the universal theme that needs to be expressed, however masked in your story.

## *City Slickers* Is Pretty Slick

As we continue the topic of using universal themes in writing, I want to talk a little about universality. Having a theme is great, but if a lot of people can't relate to it, you're not going to interest readers. You want your themes to have universal appeal—which means they should be common to the human condition. If your theme is weak and simplistic, it won't have impact. But if you build it over the entire novel, weaving it in as your characters experience life and learn and grow, the theme will deepen and become entrenched in the heart of the story.

As you plot out your scenes, you'll want to always ask yourself how you can tie your theme into that "high" moment (more on that in the section on scenes) in some way, however subtly or blatantly. It's not so much the universality of the theme, though, that determines how powerful an effect it will have; it's how well you develop it throughout your story.

## A Great Theme Will Make You Laugh and Cry

*City Slickers* is another movie chock-full of theme. Not many comedy movies do such a brilliant job of juxtaposing humor with heavy issues, but *City Slickers* is a gem of an example. Half the time you don't know whether to laugh or cry—if you're paying attention.

There are two big themes happening in this movie. The most obvious is related to Mitch, Phil, and Ed and their midlife crises. They go off on adventures and try to find thrills to offset the growing truth that they are not getting any younger and maybe the best of life has passed them by. Mitch voices the problem when he says, "What if this is the best I'll ever look, the best I'll ever be, the best I'll ever do—and it's not very good?" The theme, then, is: How do we find true meaning and happiness in life? Is it something we need to look for outside . . . or inside ourselves? Can true happiness be found, or do we have to settle for a mediocre life and learn to live with it? This major theme is closely tied up with the second one, and by answering the latter, the former is solved.

## The Secret of Happiness

The second theme is presented by Curly, the trail boss. In his enigmatic way, he looks hard at Mitch and says, "Do you want to know what the secret of happiness is?" Mitch says yes, and Curly holds up his finger. "It's this," Curly says. "One thing." "What? Your finger?" Mitch asks. Curly explains the secret of happiness is different for each person—you have to go figure what it is, but when you do, you'll know it—and you'll be happy. And you could fairly say that the pointing of his finger is a recurring visual symbol in the movie that has deep meaning,

It may sound trite and simple, but when the three friends run into real danger and have to make tough choices, they find that being true to who they are and what they believe in is what leads them to their "one thing." For Mitch, it's risking his life to save Norman, the calf, as he's swept downriver. Yet, it's bigger than that. Mitch is suffering from feeling unimportant, that his life is meaningless, makes no difference to anyone, doesn't matter. But when he saves Norman, his act mattered—maybe just to a cow, but the symbolism to Mitch is huge. He made a decision and gave it all he had because he believed it was the right thing to do. He wasn't standing on the sidelines anymore but engaging in life.

Ed deals with his anger at his delinquent father, and Phil deals with his compromised and squelched life. Their problems aren't miraculously solved by going on a cattle drive, but they do learn the true secret of happiness—and it has nothing to do with seeking out the greatest adventure or challenge "out there." They discover, to their surprise, that happiness is in the last place they would ever imagine—inside them.

Rather than look outside to find happiness, Mitch learns that he needed to change his attitude. "I'm just going to do everything better," he tells his wife when he gets home. There's a bit of Zen philosophy here—the "collect water, chop wood" realization that joy can be found in simple mundane tasks, because even those kinds of tasks have value.

## Humans Do Have a Purpose

There's an interesting little bit at the end, when the three friends bring in the herd, to the surprise of the cattle ranchers. When Mitch, Ed, and Phil are told the cows are going to market to be butchered and wrapped in plastic, they get upset. But they're told, "It's not like those cows have anything to live for. This is what they're bred for; they're not an endangered species." Mitch jokes: "Well, Phil doesn't have anything to live for either, but we're not going to kill him." This is a nice subtle tie-in with the movie's theme, implying that we humans do have purpose—we're meant for more than mindless wandering from one place to another. And just as those cows have their place in the universe, so we too have a place—we only need to look inward and find out what it is.

Did this movie make it big because of the brilliant script and fantastic humor? No doubt. But the rich themes took it to a much higher level, making it not just another funny movie.

Think about . . . watching *Babe*. If for some reason you're embarrassed to do so, say it's for a writing exercise—which it is. But take a look at the themes at work and pay attention to the symbolism. Think of a symbol you could use in your novel to tie in with your theme.

Think about how you can gradually build your theme over your novel. Consider having your protagonist or another major character in the book present the opposing view to the theme message you want to convey and come up with scene ideas in which you can have this character gradually step over to the other camp. And treat yourself to watching *City Slickers*, even if (like me) you've seen it a dozen times.

## Chapter 23: What's Your Motif?

*"Words are but symbols for the relations of things to one another and to us."*
~Friedrich Nietzsche

Because motif has some similarity to theme, I would be remiss if I left out a discussion about motif. We've just discussed the topic of theme by looking at some of my favorite movies, and now would be a good time to look at motifs. Not many writers consciously plan out motifs to use in their novel, but sometimes they come naturally into the story. Motifs are symbolic elements packed with inference, but they don't have to appear in your story as an actual item. Motifs can be a word or phrase, a concept, an image—just about anything that can be repeated with significance and symbolism. The weather can be a motif, for example, if each time something terrible is about to happen, lightning literally strikes.

Using motifs in writing fiction is one of the most powerful and evocative ways of getting across your themes in your novel. Few authors use them, and few use them well. My favorite novels of all time are ones that use motifs beautifully throughout their novel, and these elements weaving through their stories tend to stay with me for months and years after I've read the book. Why is that, and just what are motifs and how can they be utilized effectively in fiction?

## A Splash of Color

Two definitions of motif in *Merriam-Webster's* give a good feel for what a motif is: "a dominant idea or central theme; a single or repeated design or color." Think about a motif as a splash of color that you are adding to your story palette—a very noticeable, specific color that appears from time to time and that "blends in" beautifully with the overall picture you are painting. As an example, you could say that I just introduced a motif in this discussion by using the concept of color to emphasize my theme.

Motifs can be combined in your novel to create richness. I like to have at least two or three motifs woven in my novel, and I'll give you an example by referring to my contemporary women's fiction/mystery *Conundrum*.

## Motifs with Double Meanings

In *Conundrum*, my protagonist, Lisa, is searching to uncover the truth regarding her father's bizarre death twenty-five years earlier. Her interest and effort is prompted by her brother's suicidal bipolar disorder, which she believes is exacerbated by the myths and burdens surrounding their father's death. So as Lisa embarks on this journey, I brought into play a number of motifs.

The first is obvious—the word *conundrum*, which is the overall theme and serves as the title. The best use of a motif is in your title, and a great title will tie in with your book's theme, often as both a motif and a double meaning. for example—Jodi Picoult's book titles often do this, as seen in *Saving Faith* (faith being both the girl character's name and hinting at her need of being saved) and *Plain Truth* (where *plain* refers to the Amish people by that name as well as the book's plot wherein the plain truth needs to be revealed in the case of a mysterious murder among the Amish). So, in *Conundrum*, I open the novel with an actual word conundrum, one that has great symbolism to Lisa's quest. She tells of how she and her brother told conundrums through their teen years, and then I introduce a specific conundrum that serves as another motif in the book.

## Motifs Bring Cohesion

Lisa's father's expertise was in Boolean algebra. Lisa discovers a conundrum based on that algebraic formula of "and, or, or not." What I did, then, was take two motifs—the conundrum and the father's profession—and found a way to tie them together, which is a great thing to do. Throughout the novel, Lisa comes across clues that make her think "and, or, or not." Her quest is one big conundrum, and the next motif comes from the actual conundrum she found—where two guards each stand in front of a door, each claiming they guard the door to enlightenment, but one is lying and one is telling the truth. The conundrum requires the puzzle-solver to figure out which door really does lead to enlightenment. You can imagine why I was so thrilled to run across this conundrum, as it represented Lisa's search for truth (enlightenment) but with the confusion of not just many doors but many guards claiming they were telling the truth.

I hope you can see here the motifs at work and how, throughout a novel, these can surface to bring cohesion to a story. You can use an object, like a balloon for example, to symbolize important qualities. A balloon could represent freedom, the need for release. A slow-growing tree could represent faithfulness, steadfastness through all seasons, something a character can be viewing out her window at different times in her life. One of my favorite books, *The Art of Racing in the Rain*, uses the motif of race-car driving throughout the book as metaphor and symbolism.

## Motifs Tie in with Theme

In *To Kill a Mockingbird*, the bird itself is a great motif. It comes to represent the idea of innocence; thus, to kill one is to destroy innocence. This ties in beautifully with the book's themes and plot involving guilt vs. innocence (with layers of meaning, including a legal one). After Tom Robinson is shot, Mr. Underwood compares his death to "the senseless slaughter of songbirds," and at the end Scout voices that hurting Boo Radley would be like "shootin' a mockingbird."

Perhaps the most significant use of this motif is the scene in which Miss Maudie explains to Scout: "Mockingbirds don't do one thing but . . . sing their hearts out for us. That's why it's a sin to kill a mockingbird." That Jem and Scout's last name is Finch (another type of small bird) indicates that they are particularly vulnerable in the racist world of Maycomb, which often treats the fragile innocence of childhood harshly. I'm sure Harper Lee used this motif very deliberately.

I talked about the movie *K-Pax* earlier when discussing theme. A great motif is woven throughout that movie, and I recommend you watch it and pay attention to the use of light. The symbolism of light also works as a theme, as the metaphor of light (enlightenment, pureness, clarity, the light of truth being uncovered) works thematically on many levels in this movie. In almost every scene with Prot, there is some unusual treatment of light. This is because Prot claims to have come to earth on a beam of light. He is sensitive to the harsh "light" (read: truth) of our world. The pain of Earth's inhabitants is hard to take. He wears dark sunglasses in most of the scenes and is relieved when the doctor dims the lights and lowers the blinds. It's a brilliant infusion of a motif that adds richness to the movie.

With all this in mind, as you plot out your novel, or tackle your rewrite, think of two or three motifs you can weave in, then go back through your book and place them strategically. If you can somehow use the motif in your title, even better. And if you can think of motifs that parallel and/or enhance your overall theme, you will have a book that will be unforgettable. Pay attention as you read great novels to see if you can spot the motifs the author has used. You will be surprised how you will start seeing them if you pay attention and look for them. May these thoughts spark some ideas in your head and get you running to your pages!

> Think about . . . coming up with some motifs for your novel. If you already have some in place, think of other spots in other scenes where you can use that motif again. Take a look at those favorite novels you've set aside and see if you can find some motifs the authors used in their story to touch the reader's heart.

Now that we've covered the main elements of your novel, and how they speak to the heart of your story, we're going to take a break and go into scene structure. Why? Because scenes are the actual heartbeats of your story, and each scene must pulse steady, strong, and with a high peak or moment in order to lead your reader through the dark mine to the mother lode waiting at the end of the journey. Each well-crafted scene is one step further into the mine leading to the heart.

Without properly constructed scenes, your mine will collapse. No pulse—no life. It's that simple.

# Part Four: Scenes—The Heartbeats of Your Story

## Chapter 24: The Essence of a Scene

*"Life isn't a matter of milestones but of moments."*
~Rose Kennedy

Picture an EKG machine attached to a patient in a hospital. When the heart is beating steadily, each beat is shown by a spike (well, two—but I'm thinking about the bigger one) in the line running in measured time along the screen. That spike represents the moment the heart beats, indicating life and health. In your novel, each scene pulses through the heart of your story, bringing life and vigor to it, and like the peak on the EKG screen, you want each scene to have a peak—a telling, powerful moment. Strung together, these dozens of scenes tell a story of health. If your scenes are weak, aimless, without a point (pun intended), your novel will flatline. The doctors will shake their heads sadly, and the nurse will roll the gurney out to the elevator, and the last stop for your novel will be the morgue.

To get to the heart of your story—to make it through that long, dark tunnel to the mother lode buried in the mountain—you have to have a strong and steady heartbeat as you trek. So, too, your novel needs to beat strong with every scene, giving vigor and life to your story.

## Defining a Scene

I like the way Jordan Rosenfeld in her book *Make a Scene* defines what a scene is: "Scenes are capsules in which compelling characters undertake significant actions in a vivid and memorable way that allows the events to feel as though they are happening in real time." Read that a few times and let it sink in. The words that you want to pay special attention to are *compelling, significant*, and *real time.* I'll elaborate more on this in a bit.

I can attest that the biggest flaw I see in the manuscripts that I critique and edit is poor scene structure. I don't think many writers have fully explored the topic to the extent that they plan out a scene with enough understanding and craft tools to be able to really make each scene the most powerful and effective that it can be. Often scenes seem to be thrown together, starting in a place and in a manner that really doesn't work. And so, since each scene is like a mini novel (or should be), I want to talk a bit about them, and particularly about scene beginnings, since they parallel your novel beginning in many ways.

## How Would I Define a Scene?

If someone asked you to define what a scene is, what would you say? If you think about it, it's not easy to define. We tend to know when a scene works and when it doesn't. Here are some elements that are said to make up a scene that I've found in books on scene writing:

- The sum of myriad elements that work together [hmm, that's a bit vague].
- It starts and ends with a character arriving and leaving [sometimes, but not often].
- It can be a single location with many people coming and going.
- It gives the sensation that a character is "trapped" in this moment and must go through it.

I'm not all that ecstatic about these points. They don't really tell what a scene is. But let's look at what Rosenfeld said in that statement defining a scene.

## What Is Real Time?

Well, it's not backstory. I already gave spiel about leaving backstory out of your story, so let's focus on this concept of "real time." Too many manuscripts start off with either pages of narrative to set up the book or maybe only a catchy (or not) first paragraph or two that puts the protagonist right in a scene in real time—meaning they are experiencing something that, for them, is happening *right then.* Not a memory, not a flashback, not even them thinking about what is happening to them right now. But after these short moments of establishing the character in a "happening" scene, the author lapses into telling the reader important things they should know (backstory). Even if you are going to go heavily into your character's head, you need that character to be doing it "here and now" in some sort of "capsule" (as Rosenfeld says) that is unfolding in the moment. It's not all that complicated, but writers really need to resist the urge to stop the moment or veer off elsewhere.

Remember the image of the playwright getting on stage and the audience throwing tomatoes at her as she stops the play with her explanations? 'Nuff said.

## Working on Your Opening Scene

So, if you've pulled on your reins and disciplined yourself to construct that opening scene with your protagonist in a moment in real time, you now have the structure to show that character undertaking *significant* actions in a vivid and memorable way. By now you have your themes and MDQs all worked out, and you've figured out how to hint at these, along with showing your character's glimpse of greatness and core need. You've set up their persona that they show to the world, and you've hinted at their true essence underneath.

Are you starting to feel a bit overwhelmed? You might be. Not a whole lot of authors can whip up a first scene intuitively and off the cuff that contains every little element needed. And that's why the First-Page Checklist is really helpful. Once you rough in that first scene, go through and make sure you've got all the bases covered. Which begs the question. . .

## Just How Long Should a Scene Be?

I've actually read articles and book chapters that suggest certain numbers of pages, and it's not that formulaic. Genre can be a factor, since a fast-action thriller may have short, terse chapters whereas a thoughtful literary work may have long ones. The real answer, which may not be so helpful, is that a scene should be as long as it needs to be (the same is true for a novel's length). I determine the length of the scene by writing it and making sure it reaches its objective. And once it's done that, it should end. And that "objective" is *the determining* point to constructing scenes.

## Creating "Moments" So You Don't Bore Your Reader

Think about each scene as an encapsulated moment for your character that plays out in real time and reveals something significant.

Actress Rosalind Russell was asked: "What distinguishes a great movie?" She answered, "Moments." And that's so true for scenes. We remember great scenes because they contain a great moment in them. Often that moment is not something huge and explosive. On the contrary—the best moments are the very subtle ones in which the character learns or realizes something that may appear small to the outside world but is giant in scope to the character.

## It's All about the Moment

No doubt you can think of great movie moments, such as in *Casablanca* (too many in there to list!) when Ilsa tells Sam to "play it again." Or when Scout meets Boo in *To Kill a Mockingbird.* Or in *City Slickers* when Billy Crystal's character is holding up his finger to indicate the meaning of life. One of my favorite moments is in *Babe*, when Farmer Hoggett at the end of the sheep trials looks at Babe and says, "That'll do, pig."

Of course, these moments have been set up so when they play out they're powerful, but you want to think how *in every scene* you must have some moment. This is what you're building to—either some revelation of plot or of character.

## Just Why Is Your Character There?

Maybe you've put together this first scene. Ask: Why is your character there? What's her reason or need to be in that place, in that moment? What do you plan to reveal in that scene that is significant and important? These questions are especially important to consider when constructing your first scene because, as you now understand, you have to set up the visible goal and the MDQ for the *entire book*.

You need to pick a moment that will do this the best way. Too often the first few scenes of a novel aren't doing this. The protagonist is off doing something, talking to someone, and nothing is really happening—at least nothing significant. There are no high moments and no natural sense of conclusion to those scenes. Writers may feel this is the way to show the "everyman" character in his ordinary world, but as I discussed earlier, that is just plain *boring*.

## Don't Go Nowhere Fast

Scenes must have a point to them or they shouldn't be in your novel. I'll repeat that. Scenes must have a point to them or they shouldn't be in your novel. I discussed the need to find your "moment" and build to it, and the first scene really needs a kicker of a moment to hook the reader. Too many scenes are poorly structured, but there's really an easy way to look at them. And this applies to all the scenes in your novel—not just the opening scene.

## Each Scene Is a Mini Novel

There it is—the basic structure. If you think about each scene as a mini novel, you can plan them out accordingly. Each scene, like a novel, needs a beginning, middle, and end. A scene needs to have a point. It needs to build to a high moment, and then resolve in some way. (Although with a scene, you can leave the reader hanging. Okay, a lot of writers do this at the end of their novels too, to make you run out and buy the next installment, but I find that a bit annoying. I want a novel to end satisfactorily and wrap up the major story line.) What you then have with your novel is a string of mini novels that all work as nice, tidy capsules put together to paint a big picture.

Think about . . . spending some time coming up with a situation that can launch your protagonist headfirst into his story, and focus on the moment that you want to build to. If you already have a first scene written, examine it to see if it's really working. If you're not sure, think of three other possible settings and/or situations you can place your character in that might help intensify the moment you need to effectively detonate your novel. Make sure it's a terrific one, because, as you've learned, many agents and editors (and readers) won't read past the first few paragraphs.

Also, look at some great scenes in your favorite novels. Jot down how the scene opens, how long it is, where it ends, and note if the character is in an encapsulated moment that unfolds in real time and that reveals something significant. Great scenes will do just that.

## Chapter 25: Beginnings, Muddles, and Endings

*"Life is not so much about beginnings and endings as it is about going on and on and on. It is about muddling through the middle."*

~Anna Quindlen

No, that's not a typo. Middles are muddles, but I'll get into that in just a bit. We're going to break down scenes and take a deep look at them, for in order to construct a scene that beats strong and has that high moment, we have to know how to set it up. So let's take a look at each section of a scene and see what it needs—and it's fairly simple. Just as a novel needs specific things brought out in the first chapters of the story, complications in the middle, and a strong climax and resolution at the end, so do scenes.

### The Burden of the Beginning

Scene beginnings have a tremendous burden. In every opening paragraph of every scene you present to your reader you are making a promise or offering an invitation. You are promising to deliver—to entertain, impart enthralling information, move them emotionally. They have bought (or free-downloaded or borrowed) your book out of the hundreds of thousands of other novels available and are devoting their precious hours to reading your novel, so they are expecting that commitment on their part to pay off. If you open a scene with a promise to deliver and you fail to deliver, they are not going to be happy.

Avid fans of a particular author may stick with a boring scene, and maybe read even all the way to the end, in hopes the novel will pull through and come out shining. But most readers are not that gracious and forgiving. So you want to make sure you deliver. Here are a few points about scene beginnings:

- They don't have to start at a "beginning," such as the start of a day (too many characters waking up when the alarm clock goes off). The beginning can and often should be in the middle of something already happening.

- They need a hook. Not just your opening scene but every scene needs a hook to draw the reader in, chapter after chapter. If you start off with boring narrative, you're not going to hook them.

- Each scene launch is a reintroduction. Ask—where did I last leave those characters and what were they doing? You need to make the passing of time clear, and if it's been a few scenes since we've seen those characters, you'll need a bit of a reminder in the beginning of the scene to connect to that last moment.

- Just as with the first scene in your novel, you want to get your POV character into the scene ASAP (and in real time). The points that apply to your book's opening scene mostly apply to every scene.

- Start an action without explaining anything.

- Give a nod to setting (a nod, not a treatise).

### Going Nowhere Fast

Here's what literary agent Donald Maass says: "You would be surprised in how many middle scenes in how many manuscripts there seems to be no particular reason for a character to go somewhere, see someone, learn something, or avoid something." (And at his week-long workshop he really grumbled about the plethora of scenes where two people are sitting around drinking tea.) You don't want this to happen in your novel.

## Muddle the Middle of Your Scenes

Just as middle scenes of a novel can slog along and sag, so too middles of a scene can drag or not go anywhere. Knowing your high moment will really help avoid that. One good way to have compelling middles is to work backward from your high moment. If you know, for example, that Mary thinks George has taken her out to dinner to propose, but the high moment reveals he's breaking up with her, you can picture that instant of her being stunned and think how she is going to feel right before that. You want your character to change in some small way by the end of the scene, and so think how Mary feels ten, twenty, or thirty minutes before this shocking moment. How is she going to be feeling twenty minutes after? You want to start the scene with her expectations and in the middle of action—either already at the restaurant or pretty close to being there. In your middle, you don't want to spend a lot of time (or maybe even any time) driving there or getting your character from any one place to another. Don't drag the middle by stretching time (unless it serves a purpose in the scene to do so).

## Complicate, Exacerbate

Middles of novels are where you up the stakes, complicate and confound your character, make things worse. You might add danger or reveal a surprise twist. A middle is the unveiling of the story line. In each scene, as you build to your moment, you want to do the same. Add complications, obstacles, twists. Maybe Mary's car doesn't start and she's late meeting George at the restaurant, which adds to her anxiety. Maybe Mary gets a phone call right before she leaves that complicates the (complementary) subplot regarding her friend who's going through a divorce. That can enrich the scene as Mary thinks how lucky she is to have George and how he's going to propose to her in a few minutes.

If you are going to throw a twist into your scene, such as George breaking up with Mary instead of proposing to her, you can use the middle to set up Mary's expectations of one outcome, only to have a reversal at the high point. Reversals are terrific, and if you put in at least three things leading up to them that indicate the opposite outcome (such as Mary's expectation that George is going to propose), they will be powerful.

## Endings That Spark Beginnings

Finally, let's look at endings. Just like beginnings, endings carry a special burden. The reader must be left with a feeling, like an aftertaste. You need to stop and think: What feeling do I want the reader to have? Shock, sadness, warmth, confusion, curiosity? You want to keep in mind that the basic storytelling structure for a novel is action—reaction—action—reaction. Too many scenes end with a character experiencing something and then . . . it ends. We need to see how the character *reacts* to what has just happened. You don't have to do this every time, and in some genres where plot is king (suspense/thrillers), you might end with the building exploding, and the reader has no idea if your character just died. But as a general rule, you want to be with your character and see their reaction, feeling, or response—even if told in one line—to what has just happened.

## Endings Need to Feel Like Endings

A scene ending needs to feel just like that—an ending. There must be a sense of completion, even if the reader is left hanging. Even if the POV character is left confused in the middle of something, the scene itself has to have a feeling of completeness in that the scene wholly accomplished its objective—leading you from one place to another, from one moment to another. The ending must leave the reader with a sense of anticipation and a desire to read on. Each ending, in essence, should spark a new beginning. That's accomplished by giving the reader a piece of new plot information, presenting another clue, or revealing something moving or fascinating about the character that makes them care what happens next. Again, moments don't need to be big. They are powerful and impacting if they contain meaning for your character.

Have you ever read a novel late at night, telling yourself you are only going to read to the end of the chapter, but then when you hit the last line, you are so gripped you just have to read *one more* chapter? You can't wait to find out what happens next, even though you really need to sleep. There's nothing more satisfying for a writer than to be told by a reader that she stayed up until five a.m. finishing your novel because the scenes were that riveting.

## Two Types of Endings

There are basically two types of endings of scenes—plot endings and character endings. Plot endings might be cliffhangers or contain a new plot twist or reveal a clue. A character ending is more about insight. The reader now knows something more about your character, or you may have the character thinking about what just happened, or you may have some poignant dialog (even one line) or description (motif or metaphor) that your character ponders. Think about zooming in like a camera to your character's thoughts and feelings. Or maybe zoom out to show a larger understanding your character now has for her life or her world. Moments of insight make for powerful endings.

Think about . . . choosing a random scene in your WIP (work in progress) and check to see if you have all you need in your opening paragraphs as noted in the above chapters. If you are missing some things, put them in. If you need to rework the entire scene so you can have a terrific beginning, then do that. And don't forget to keep the "moment" in mind so you will build up to it.

Look at not just your first scene's middle but those of random scenes in your novel. Find the high points and see if you have developed the middle so that it is leading to that moment and complicating things. See if you can add in expectations that imply the opposite outcome. If your character expects something bad to happen, have three things in the middle that imply her instincts will prove right. Then when that bad thing doesn't happen, it will pack a punch.

Look at your scene endings and see if they wrap up the scene like the ending of a good book. If they stop abruptly, think how you can create either a plot revelation or a character insight to end smoothly and leave the reader wanting more.

# Part Five: Adding a Little More Heart to Your Story

## Chapter 26: The Heart of Your Setting

*"Some of our most exquisite murders have been domestic, performed with tenderness in simple, homey places like the kitchen table."*
~Alfred Hitchcock

While delving into the heart of your story, I've only touched a little on setting. Setting is so important to your book, and all too often writers practically ignore it in their quest to unveil a great plot or take the reader on a character's journey.

But stop and think for a moment about yourself and the world you live in. Each moment you're alive, you are interacting with your setting. At times, where you are is inconsequential and unimportant to what is going on in your life at that moment. You could be in a coffee shop, at the top of a mountain, or waiting at the dentist's office to get your teeth cleaned and it wouldn't matter in respect to what you may be going through, feeling, thinking, or desiring at the time. Much of our lives we are in mundane places, doing mundane things. But do readers want to read about that? Do you recall what I said a few chapters ago about books that portray ordinary people? I said ordinary people are boring—and so are mundane, boring settings. No one wants boring.

So, does that mean in every scene in your book you must have a unique and fascinating setting so as to keep the reader from being bored? Of course not. If we did that, the setting would be screaming, and the reader would have trouble hearing what the characters have to say.

If you want to portray a character living a normal kind of life, you are going to have scenes where you show her in fairly ordinary settings—like her kitchen, or at the grocery store, or walking down a sidewalk. There will be times when your setting is just a backdrop to the scene unfolding. You may have an intense confrontational dialog happening at restaurant or on the beach, and you want the focus to be on what's being said, and how the characters are interacting. That's all well and good. But when you also weave the setting in with what else is going on in the scene, and choose a setting that will enhance what's going on with your characters, you will add richness and texture to your novel.

## Put Your Characters in a Place on Purpose

I want to urge you to stop and think before you create a scene: Where is the best place I can put my character to have this scene unfold and lead to the important moment revealed in this scene? Rather than pick something off the top of your head, which is what a lot of writers do in their rush to put a scene down, you will find that if you deliberately and judiciously choose a setting that will best serve the interests of your plot and your character's need for that scene, you will have a much more powerful novel. Once you learn some great tips and techniques about setting, I hope you will see the importance of doing this, and enjoy the challenge as well.

There are so many ways to deal with setting, and so I'm going to take a few pages to go into the exploration of this topic and show you ways you can utilize setting and bring it alive for your characters (or rather, have your characters bring the setting alive).

Setting can be a great tool to reveal a character's mind-set and mood. You can use setting as a vehicle or trigger to aid your plot. By putting your character in a specific place, you can make certain things happen that will enrich your story—you can go so far as to have the setting a motif or symbol as well. If you have two people sitting around talking while drinking tea (I hear Donald Maass scream, "No, no, no!"), you might think of a better setting in which to put your old ladies so that something can happen or influence their conversation or interfere with them to add complication to the story, or to reveal something important about one character's personality, needs, fears, or dreams.

## Places in Your Past That Evoke Feeling

Think about some places in your past. Maybe a place from childhood that you visit once in a while—a place that stirs memory. Even a similar place can evoke memories, and so settings can evoke emotions and memories in your characters as well. In some novels, setting is almost the star of the show, like Pat Conroy's *The Prince of Tides*. In books like this, the way the characters interact with their setting is crucial to the story. Many authors are known for their books set in a particular town or locale. But if you are not writing that kind of book, you may think that setting really isn't important at all. And it may be that the kind of novel you are writing could be set pretty much anywhere, or in any small town or large city.

With many of my novels I pondered long and hard as to where I should set the story. Oftentimes I knew I needed a city backdrop, but which city? With *Intended for Harm*, my modern-day Bible rendition of Jacob and Joseph, I waffled back and forth between Los Angeles and San Francisco—two cities I was very familiar with. But I decided to go with LA because I'd grown up there and felt I could capture the era of 1971 to present day the best by drawing from my own experiences and memories. But I could have set that novel in any city. Yet, once I made that choice, I knew I would have to make that setting live inside my characters as they lived there in my story.

You may choose a familiar place in which to set your novel, and we've all heard the line about how we should only write about what we know (which I don't agree with—we should only write what we've researched well). But when we write about a place we know, we can save ourselves a lot of work researching, and we can often bring believability to that place because of our experience there. What I'd like you to think about, though, as you dive deep into setting, is how certain places make you *feel* and why. We link setting to events in our lives, and those events contain an emotional content.

## Use Your Setting to Highlight Theme and Character

When choosing settings for your scenes, you want to think about the kinds of places that will allow the emotions, needs, dreams, and fears of your characters to come out. Certain places will trigger these things to come to the surface and will stir memories. Your character has a past, and even if she never visits any of the places in her past in your novel, other places can draw out feelings and memories. This happens to us all the time.

Of course, if you are putting your characters in places they've been before, or the same town they've been living in their whole life, those memories and feelings are closer to the surface. The point is, you want to use your setting to help bring out your themes, drive your plot, and reveal character. You don't have to do this, but by ignoring setting you are missing out on a great tool in your writer's toolbox that you can use in a powerful way.

Earlier I had you think about the places in your past that evoked special memories or feelings. There will be moments in your novel when you want your character to realize something, learn something, change in some way, be affected profoundly. You can call setting into play in these instances. You want the protagonist's relationship to her world to grab you. And you can bring her world alive with rich detail by showing her world through her eyes and the effect that world has on her.

## Ask Your Character

Here are some questions you can ask regarding the setting your character finds herself in, whether it's the overall setting of the novel or a particular place in a particular scene you want to write:

- What might be special about this place that a person passing through might not notice?
- How does she feel when she is there?
- What memory or emotion does the place evoke in her and why? Can you come up with something that happened there that ties in with the wound from her past? To a hope or dream she may have had but lost somewhere along the way?
- How does she look at not just the place but the kind of life she has there (professional, family, community)?

- What is her one special secret place she likes to go to and what does she do there?
- What is the one place she avoids and would never go to?
- What can she notice while she is there that no one else notices?
- What special thing can you have happen in this special place that reveals something secret about her? About her dreams? About her fears?
- What one memory can you come up with that is triggered by her being in this place?
- What was her happiest moment in this place? Her saddest?
- If she has come back after a period of time, how has this place changed for her, and how does that change make her feel? Happy, sad, nostalgic, fearful?
- What conflicting feelings does she have about being there?

## Setting That Triggers Memories

One novel that comes to my mind in posing these questions is Barbara Kingsolver's *Animal Dreams.* This book is all about a character who is dealing with setting. Her protagonist has returned to the town she grew up in after many years. Throughout the novel as she deals with her senile father, the neighbors she thought she knew, and her memories that come back to haunt her, we watch how this place and her past assault and change her radically. It's a book all about how setting can trigger change and awareness. How it can make us step back and assess our present lives in the light of our past.

So, as you think about setting for your novel overall and for individual scenes, think about the themes you are bringing out. Think about not just the plot points the setting can help reveal but also the deep character traits that can be triggered by locale and environment. We like to stroll down memory lane—both figuratively and literally. Sometimes we do it out of a masochistic desire to feel hurt or pain, or to wallow in painful memories. Other times it's out of nostalgia, to try to capture a feeling we somehow lost along the way. These are things your characters can do too. They are human things we humans do.

So when you get ready to write a scene, don't just plop your character in the closest coffee shop down the street. First think about what you need to reveal in the scene. Then think of the best place to put your character so that this moment in the scene will be enhanced or triggered by the setting. Let her look at something she's seen before but in a different way. Then watch what happens.

## Seeing the World through Your Character's Eyes

One of the essential things you need to do in your first scene particularly is ground your protagonist in her setting. Just writing that made me blow out a breath. Why? Because I edit and critique many manuscripts that contain really dull narrative about the setting. Most common is the scene that goes underway for a paragraph or two and then suddenly inserts an author interruption in which I read a number of paragraphs (or pages) telling all kinds of details about the scenery, locale, and the world the protagonist is in. The problem is this information is all detached from the POV character. The world must always be seen through your character's eyes, not be described to the reader by the author in an info dump.

### Show *Her* World

At some point you made a decision to set your story in a particular locale and time period. And in choosing your first scene you thought of a specific place, time of year, time of day (or at least you should have). I read one best-selling novel (which was near the top of my "worst books" list) that didn't even tell the reader what part of the US the story was set in until somewhere around page 150, and it only said "the South." There was no sense of place, and certainly not in the protagonist's POV.

Maybe your plot is highly dependent upon your locale, as many novels are. The setting is often like a character, evoking the South, for example (*Gone with the Wind* or *The Secret Life of Bees*) or a particular country or a type of natural environment like the wilderness or the Arctic Circle. But whether or not the actual location is intrinsically tied in with your plot, you want the setting to be experienced and expressed by your character—not by you, the author. Remember—playgoers don't come to the show to hear the playwright; they want to watch the play. And so it is with a novel.

## What Makes Setting Special for Your Character?

That's the question you should be asking—not just for your first scene but in all your scenes. As you think about beginning your novel and putting your character somewhere in some time, stop and think about how she *feels* about being there. Once you can tap into how she interacts with the place in which she lives, works, and grows, you're halfway there. You want to show the scenery not just through her eyes but with an emotional response. Once you do that, your setting will become alive and vibrant.

I mentioned earlier a book that I think is one of the most powerful books in terms of evoking setting: Pat Conroy's *The Prince of Tides*. The book oozes with setting, and it's so intertwined with his characters that you feel you are there, sensing what they sense and experiencing the locale in a truly deep and personal way. Conroy doesn't accomplish this by writing pages of description.

Sure, there's a lot of description of Colleton, SC. How is it I remember the name of that place after having read that book two decades ago? Because he made me feel as if I'd lived there. And his narrative writing is evocative and beautiful (which is important too). But his descriptions work because they are so enmeshed with his protagonist, Tom Wingo, that you can feel it. The best way to avoid a big information dump every time you introduce a new place is to feel, see, hear, smell, and emotionalize the setting in your character's POV.

Think about . . . places you've lived. Try to lock on to a few memories of very specific spots, like a park or school playground, that is linked to a powerful memory. Maybe it's a very ordinary place that wouldn't mean anything to anyone else but it holds a special meaning for you. Think of a place where you felt hurt, where something happened that upset you, where an embarrassing or hurtful incident occurred. Close your eyes and see what you notice about the details about that place.

If you have a scene to write, ask the questions above and try to pick a setting that will be perfect for what your scene needs to accomplish. If you are in the rewrite stage and you have a flat or boring scene set in a boring place, think of a new setting in which to unfold this scene, and pick something that will trigger a feeling or memory in your character that will help advance the plot or reveal something significant about your character.

## Chapter 27: Space and Time

*"Clocks slay time . . . time is dead as long as it is being clicked off by little wheels; only when the clock stops does time come to life."*
~William Faulkner

Sol Stein, the famous editor, author, and writing instructor, has a very short chapter in his classic book *Stein on Writing* that he calls "Creating the Envelope." As I looked through my numerous books on writing craft, I drifted toward his book (which happens a lot), and was reminded again of the best advice to give writers regarding setting details. I discussed in the last chapter of exploring your character's feelings and responses to setting, to make setting personal and dynamic in your novel, as well as to give it heart. There's nothing more boring in a novel than a paragraph of dry narrative to describe each new place your character finds himself in (well, it's up there with trite dialog). But in this chapter I want to talk about boiling down the essence of a locale or setting in a scene, and Stein's "envelope" really is the best way to do it.

Here's what he says: "Writing fiction is a delicate balance. On the one hand, so much inexperienced writing suffers from generalities. The writer is urged to be specific, particular, concrete at the same time. When the inexperienced writer gives the reader detail on character, clothing, settings, and actions, he tends to give us a surfeit, robbing the reader of one of the great pleasures of reading: exercising the imagination. My advice on achieving a balance is to . . . err on the side of too little rather than too much. For the reader's imagination, less is more."

## Less Really Is More

I've often said this very phrase to my editing clients, and I really believe it's true—not just in description but in about every aspect and element in a novel. Less spoken, more implied. Less shown, more left up to the imagination. Go ahead and freewrite a page or two about a new setting your character has entered. Maybe she's just stepped out of an airport terminal in a foreign country. Play with her immediate reactions, the smells and sounds that trigger memories and make impressions. Describe everything and everyone she sees until you have the whole picture before you.

To Stein, that would be stuffing the envelope—to overflowing. And that's a great exercise to do to get your visual camera up and running. Sometimes if you close your eyes and picture your setting as if you are your character sitting on a bench or chair or some appropriate seating, you can just wait and watch things happen. You may start to hear people speak and birds call out. You may start seeing little details, like the bits of grass growing up in the cracks in the sidewalk and the way old tree roots have pushed up the concrete and made an abandoned child's tricycle sit at a funny angle.

But once you are done exploring your setting, you want to look through all those little bits in that envelope that you've dumped out on the table and pick *one or two things* that stand out. Stein says, "I have sometimes described the reader's experience to students as an envelope. It is a mistake to fill the envelope with so much detail that little or nothing is left to the reader's imagination. The writer's job is to fill the envelope with just enough to trigger the reader's imagination."

I thumbed through some novels I love when writing this chapter, and snagged some little bits of setting the authors give us:

- "Harold's place looked much like ours, flat as flat, though the house was more Victorian in style, with sunrise gable finishes and a big porch swing in front. Harold didn't have as much land as my father, but he farmed it efficiently." (Jane Smiley, *A Thousand Acres*) From that brief description she moves on to an event that took place involving Harold and his farm. You notice she only used two sentences to evoke the setting, and since the reader already knows much about her storyteller's farm, just saying his place looked "much like ours" except for a couple of small differences is enough to set the stage.

- "Leaphorn noticed it immediately—the cold, stagnant air of abandoned places. He was standing beside Thatcher when Thatcher unlocked the door to the apartment of Dr. Friedman-Barnal and pushed it open. The trapped air flowed outward into Leaphorn's sensitive nostrils. He sensed dust in it, and all that mixture of smells which humans leave behind them when they go away. The park service calls such apartments TPH, temporary personnel housing. At Chaco, six of them were build into an L-shaped frame structure on a concrete slab—part of a complex that included maintenance and storage buildings . . . a line of eight frame bungalows backed against the low cliff of Chaco Mesa." (Tony Hillerman, *A Thief of Time*) From there, Hillerman's characters enter and the scene begins, but the setting has been nicely established in just those few short lines, giving the reader a clear sense of the place, yet allowing for the reader to use much imagination to picture the details.

- " And then we fell out of the sky and into the verdant fields north of Sacramento. Stunning. absolutely stunning, the vastness of a world so intense with growth and birth, in the season of life between the dormant winter and the baking heat of summer. Vast, rolling hills covered with newly sprung grass and great swaths of wildflowers. Men working the land in their tractors, churning the soil, releasing a heady brew of smells: moisture and decay, fertilizer and diesel fumes." (Garth Stein, *The Art of Racing in the Rain*) That's pretty much all Enzo the dog tells us about his first impression of Sacramento, and of course you'd expect a dog to particularly notice both the smells of the area and all the wide-open spaces in which he'd love to run. A great example of getting into character and showing just what he might notice as opposed to what another person (or dog?) might.

## Altering the Quality of Time in Your Novel

I want to take a little detour here to talk a bit about something I love seeing done well in novels—and that's altering the quality of time. In a movie there are all kinds of techniques the director and film editor can use to speed time up and slow time down. One easy way is by slowing down the action to make everything move at a snail's pace, but writers have to find other ways to do this in a novel. Just putting in an aside to the reader to "read this passage slowly" won't work.

But I'm going to talk not just about *the speed* at which time seems to move but also about the *quality* of time. If that seems like an esoteric concept, it is. But I bet you can think of instances or moments when time has felt different to you. Not just when it slows way down (like when you've had an accident or you're waiting for a doctor to come into the exam room with your test results) or speeds up (getting old, in general) but when it *feels* different. Do you have any idea of what I'm referring to?

## Manipulate Time

Time is an element in your novel. Your story is told over a period of time, be it a few days or forty years. You pace your novel so as to have a smooth passage of time and a coherent one the reader can follow without getting tripped up (or so you hope). But handling time can also be a sort of technique you can use in your novel to evoke emotions, and maybe emotions that you can't really name or put a finger on.

Have you ever experienced a moment when someone gave you some shocking news? Maybe someone you were close to died in a tragic accident, and you sat somewhere quietly and tried to process it. Sometimes in those instances, time feels muddled, thick, hazy. You can almost give it a physical or tactile description here. Have you ever witnessed an accident—a car crash or something so unexpected that time seemed to stop until you could catch up to it? Yes, it seemed to slow down, but it also had a bright, shattering feeling. Maybe I'm just waxing poetic because it's really hard for us to put into words such a nebulous sensation such as the quality of time.

## Poignant Beauty in a Plastic Bag

Think about your character sitting on a park bench after getting some tragic news. You could write "Megan sat there, shocked, unable to move. She had no idea how much time passed before she realized her hands were numb from the cold winter air." Okay, I just *told* you how my character felt and that she lost track of time, but I didn't help you *feel* how that time passed.

Now what if you do this? Have her look around her and notice something she's never paid attention to before. Maybe a shaft of light is hitting the roof of a nearby car and refracting. Maybe her eyes catch on the leaves in the tree next to her shivering as if cold. Sometimes having a character notice something seemingly insignificant shows her inner awareness is shifting, and that often shifts the quality of time. This is a great place to insert a motif!

There's that great moment in the movie *American Beauty* with the swirling plastic bag. If you saw the movie, you know exactly which moment I'm talking about. It seems like such an odd bit—listening to Ricky (the teen boy love interest) talk as he shows Jane (his soon-to-be girlfriend) a video he took of a bag swirling in the wind. It's a pivotal and important scene in the movie because Ricky voices the big theme when he says as they're watching, "This bag was just dancing with me. Like a little kid begging me to play with it . . . for fifteen minutes. Sometimes there's so much beauty in the world, I feel I can't take it. And my heart is just going to cave in." Time, at that moment, feels so altogether different from normal. This scene slows the movie down so that this poignant moment can seep into the viewer's heart.

## An Indescribable, Visceral Thing

Besides being a brilliant moment about beauty (what's so beautiful about a boring bag swirling with leaves and dirt on the street?), while you watch the bag, the quality of time seems to change. The poignancy of the moment does something to time. And so with the girl on the bench in my little narrative. As she starts seeing things around her and noticing details that are small and which no one would pay attention to, time shifts in quality. Emphasis is put on small detail and keen observation.

If you can give the sense of heightened awareness—noticing sounds you hadn't noticed, like the birds chirping, or noticing sounds disappearing, as if everything goes hush and silent suddenly—you can change the quality of time. At least that's what I call it, and it's something I use very deliberately in pretty much all my novels at some key moment or another—particularly when I want the reader to slow down and notice something important that they might miss. Often it's not something visible, but more emotional or visceral. I won't even try to define it. But I intuitively sense when I need to grab the reader and get him to—in effect—sit and watch the leaves and bag swirling and notice the beauty in the moment. Maybe it's a Zen thing.

There are moments in life where we feel strangely and marvelously alive. And there are moments when we feel we are dead and can no longer responding to anything around us. The quality of time changes in those moments too. There are no set rules on how you can emphasize this change-in-time quality, but by having your character notice small things, which slows time down, and explore how she feels in that moment, you may find ways of expressing this very powerful effect.

A great book that spectacularly masters the nuances of time and how it feels is Ian McEwan's novel *The Child in Time*. He plays with time in that story in awesome ways (as it serves strongly as symbol and motif in the book), and the story is compelling. It's his best book, in my opinion.

Think about . . . establishing setting the way Sol Stein encourages—by putting a few little bits in the envelope and letting the reader use her imagination to supply the rest. Go through a scene or two that you've written and take a look at your description of setting. See if you can cut it down and leave just a line or two (rewrite if necessary) that not only gives the essence of your setting but provides setting that is felt by your character. Chop out any unattached narrative (meaning it isn't being observed and filtered by your POV character). Set that material aside, and if you feel there's something in there that needs to be in your novel, find another place in which to put it, and reveal those details through the eyes of your character. If you're feeling particularly ambitious, you can go also through your whole novel and highlight your passages of dry narrative to go through later with this same process.

Think of a crucial scene in your novel in which a character needs to react to something and you want to suspend the moment and give it a different time quality. Try the technique above to "slow time down" and see what happens.

# Chapter 28: The Inevitable Ending

*"If you want a happy ending, that depends, of course, on where you stop your story."*

~Orson Welles

Earlier I covered some tips about creating scenes, and most particularly in discussion about your novel's first scene. I mentioned that the first scene in your book carries a special burden, and if you've been faithfully reading this book, you'll recall we spent a large number of pages on just your first scene! Now, as we approach the end of this book, wrapping up this intensive look at writing the heart of your story, I want to shift from scene endings to *ending* scenes.

## Are You (More Than) Ready for It to End?

I promise we won't take eight chapters to go over this pivotal and crucial part of your novel, but it does require some attention. Writers tend to get a bit tired, burned out, and sometimes even a little sick of the story they've been crafting for months (years?) by the time they see the home stretch, and often they push through or rush to wrap it all up so they can figure out where they left their life, kids, and keys that seem to have gone AWOL while they were hunched over their computer. But the ending scenes carry the *next* biggest burden in your novel, and so if you're feeling the urge to hurry up and get the $%&* book done, or if you've already written an ending but it feels flat and ineffective, I'm hoping some of the suggestions I propose will be of help to you.

I recently heard the expression "Get in quickly; get out quickly." I hadn't heard that before, and it came from a critique partner who felt my fairly short wrap-up ending to my epic novel *Intended for Harm* was just right. I recognize the truth in those words, for you don't want to drag out either the beginning or the ending of your novel. A "not-so-long good-bye" might just be a good thing. But it needs to be oh-so-right, short or not.

## Oh Great—Another Burden

So, just as you have to cram in so many elements in a few short pages in the opening of your story, you also have to accomplish a number of big things in your last few pages. I really love writing the last scene in my novels. I feel it's like a reward given to me for getting to the end. And rather than looking at ending my book as a big chore with the pressure on, it's usually a high, exciting, invigorating time at my computer, filled with joy.

Of course, having done my homework in advance and jotted notes down as the novel progressed regarding what I need at the end of the book, I don't have that horrible trepidation of finishing. I'm always a bit sad to write the last line because by that point I'm so madly in love with my characters and the world I've created that I don't want to go away.

I feel like Pokey (from the old *Gumby* cartoon show), who pops out of a book and zooms away on his weird horsie feet that slide along the floor. I hate the zooming-away part. Of course, I could write a follow-up novel and drench myself in another journey with those same characters, but alas, each book must end.

So your ending takes some serious thought and planning because you have a lot of elements you need to bring out and tie up (not just plot but emotional payoffs as well). I'm not talking here about writing the climax of your book, although in some cases a climax appropriately comes in the last scene, and sometimes on the last page, of a novel. If that's the case with your novel, you have an even greater challenge because you're combining both the climax and the ending at the same time, which can be tricky. Most books tend to work best if the climax comes enough before the last scene or two to allow the reader to do some processing (and the protagonist as well) of the climax—the gigantic event or moment you spent your entire book building to (which answers the MDQ and shows whether or not the protagonist reached her visible goal).

### No Pressure—Just Do Everything on the List . . .

A. S. Byatt wrote: "We are driven by endings as by hunger." No pressure, right? How about some more pressure? Here's what you should believe (and strive to accomplish with your ending):

- Endings should be unforgettable
- Endings should satisfy both the intellect and the heart
- Endings must wrap up all the loose plot end
- Endings must clearly answer both the plot and spiritual MDQ
- Endings should highlight the novel's theme
- Endings, if possible, should somehow connect to something in your opening scenes
- Endings, if possible, should bring back a repeated motif used throughout the book
- Endings should leave a significant take-home message or feeling that is powerful and lingering

You can see here that a lot of what needs to appear in your ending won't be all that hard if you did a good job setting up those elements from page one. Readers want to feel a sense of completion at the end of your novel, that you've given them something, and that you delivered what you promised in the first scene.

## Aim for That Unforgettable Ending

All that is a tall order! But just as with the first scene, with conscious effort and forearmed with knowledge, you can create a memorable ending. Not a whole lot of books have moved me with tremendous force in the last scene. I've read some great last scenes, and many endings are truly satisfying, some even lingering with me for days after I put the book down. But I do hunger for an incredible ending that will knock my socks off. Three books with endings that blew me away are Barbara Kingsolver's *Animal Dreams* (I cried my heart out), Garth Stein's *The Art of Racing in the Rain (*yep, cried even harder, but in a gloriously happy way), and Marquez's *One Hundred Years of Solitude* (which had me gasping and delirious over how he wrapped everything he set up on *the last page*!). Don't you want to create that kind of response in your readers when they read your last pages? I do!

## Endings that Ruin Your Novel

Have you ever read a great book that carries you all the way to the end, and then the ending is so disappointing you feel cheated? I've felt that way many times, and usually it's because the ending doesn't fit the theme and story, or the characters behave so contrary to the way they been portrayed that I just don't believe it. On some occasions the author has been promising certain things, building up my anticipation, but when the moment comes, she breaks her promise and the ending falls flat.

I wonder if authors sometimes write these kinds of endings because they think they will sell more books or add more drama. One book that comes to mind (sorry if this offends anyone) is *The Horse Whisperer*, which I really did enjoy a lot. The premise and story line were great, the conflict throughout was believable, and the characters were engaging and full-dimensional. That is, until the ending. I suppose Robert Redford (who optioned, starred in, and directed the movie, from what I understand) disliked the ending too, for in the movie he came up with a new ending that really did work and was believable. I'm glad he did. I had one of those moments where I wanted to throw the book across the room while screaming, "Oh come on! You've got to be kidding."

## Keep Your Characters in Character

If you haven't read the book, what develops as the main thread of the story is a basic plot type. You have a woman (Annie) torn deciding between two men. She can either stick with her husband (Robert), whom she doesn't feel close to anymore, or go after the cowboy hunk (Tom), whom she's been spending a little too much time with. Nicolas Evans, the author, makes Tom an intriguing character. Without going into great detail about the plot, Tom is a man secure in himself, kind, principled, but very level-headed. He is not brash, emotional, or given to delusions of grandeur or lunacy. Yet, when the time comes for Annie to choose between the two men, instead of letting her make that choice herself, he forces her hand in a ridiculous act of self-sacrifice—letting a wild mustang kill him (yes, kill him!) in order to take the pressure of deciding off poor Annie. Okay, how many sane and respectable people do you know would step out in front of a car to die in order to help someone make a decision about their love life? Sorry, it's just not believable.

## Explosions Just Might Blow Up Your Book

Which brings me to the point. Don't come up with some explosive, fabulous, shocking ending to your book that is not in total harmony with your story. You make your ending dramatic by *giving it impactful meaning for your protagonist*. Do you get that? It doesn't have to be a big moment at all. In fact, some of the best novels end with a powerful, poignant, subtle moment that is quiet and understated. And yet because of the impact on the protagonist, it is huge.

I love *The Thirteenth Tale* by Diane Setterfield. Setterfield in this debut novel gives us a strong and terrific ending, but not much at all "happens." The protagonist has fallen asleep in a chair while watching over the famous author she's been interviewing over a period of months and wakes to find she's died. That's not quite the last scene, but the book ends with a whisper not a bang. Why is it so amazing? All the themes, secrets, clues, and motifs that Setterfield wove throughout the book come together at the end, as any good mystery should. Her themes are death, loss, identity, twins, reconciliation, truth—to name some. It's no surprise it hit the NY Times best-seller list as #1 only a week after its release. (And surely the beautiful writing and gripping plot had a lot to do with that.)

As a huge fan of motifs, I was so drawn to her early setting up of the twin theme, as the reader learns right at the beginning that the protagonist, Margaret, accidentally discovered she'd had a twin sister at birth she never knew about and who had died. There are lots of plot elements having to do with twins throughout (a big part of the story), but this little fact becomes a motif that pops up here and there, and then comes fully formed at the end in a poignant manner. If you haven't read this book, I highly encourage you to do so. This is a great example of a novel that shines from page one to the end.

### The Ending Serves the Plot

All this is to say, you need to have the ending of your novel *serve* your plot. It's where you bring to the spotlight all the reasons you wrote the story and all the passionate things you feel, which you infused along the way. Don't get gimmicky at the last minute—get authentic. Speak from the heart and let that be what drives the writing of your ending. Let the reader see (show it, don't tell it) how your protagonist has changed and what she's learned.

### The Inevitable Ending You Know Is Coming

As contradictory as this might sound, endings in novels need to seem inevitable without being predictable. When your reader finishes the book , she should feel that this was the *only* way it could have ended. Everything has led up to this finale, and it plays out perfectly. This isn't predictability. You don't want readers thinking they knew exactly what was going to happen and are bored as they hurriedly flip through the last pages of the book.

Recently I read a couple of award-winning sci-fi novels that were really pretty good until about the last fifty pages. I found myself starting to skim through the inevitable spaceship battles and the endings—to the point that I didn't really read the last chapters. Such a difference from Orson Scott Card's masterpiece *Ender's Game*, considered one of the all-time greatest sci-fi books written (and I agree). The surprise twist at the climax and the completely unexpected ending blew me away. Yet, I could say it was the best ending for the book, and entirely unpredictable.

## Inevitable but Predictable?

It's okay for readers to know *what* is going to happen (boy gets girl, Frodo destroys the ring), but they don't know *how*. You want enough surprises and twists that the reader is thrilled, but you don't want them throwing the book across the room upset that your ending makes no sense. One writing instructor calls the ending a "debriefing." I like to think of it as a camera pull-back in a mental way. This is where the protagonist shifts her focus from the small scope of the events in the climax to the larger purview of processing what she just went through, the decision she made, the changes she experienced, and who she is now. It's as if her gaze is wider and deeper as she looks at her new place in the story with better vision and understanding. There is a sense of an "I see now and I understand" feel.

## Reduce to the Bare Essence

I mentioned this line earlier: "Get in quickly; get out quickly." There should be a sense of boiling everything down to its purest essence. Every word of dialog, every line of description, should truly count. The end is no place for excessive narration, pontification, explanation. This is where you show a memorable moment with your character, a short but important one. Think of a dramatic play in which the narrating character sums up the story (I'm picturing *Hamlet*) after all has been said and done. You don't want to do this exactly—jumping in as the author and summing up the story they just read—but you do want to give the feeling that things are being wrapped up.

In *Conundrum*, after my protagonist, Lisa, learns a shocking truth (big plot twist/surprise) about her long-dead father, whom she has been trying to learn about throughout the course of the novel, she sits in her living room on New Year's day (hinting at new beginnings, as she is also, finally, pregnant—another new beginning). I bring in some of the motifs I've been using in the book, phrases and ideas used in important places that hold a lot of meaning for her, so as she reflects on where she is, what she's learned, how she now feels, and what she hopes for the future, it all plays out in a few short paragraphs, reprinted below (I'm going to boldface the repeated phrases and motif used since you won't know what they are):

A great sigh broke loose from inside me. I had come to the end of my father's story; I had navigated this convoluted maze and now where did that leave me? What had compelled me, those months ago, to uncover the clues to his death? Some crazy notion that I could help Raff? Where had that come from?

Perhaps my buried memories of my father, a man who had imprinted his goodness and love on my heart so long ago, had nudged me toward **truth**. Toward a need to vindicate him somehow, clear his name of the false labels slapped upon him: cowardly, suicidal, heartless. I had supposed that if I searched for him, searched hard, I could find him. And I did. At least, I believed I did.

It struck me that I had no idea where my father was buried. In Los Angeles somewhere? Or would his family have buried him in New York? I made a mental note to call my uncle Samuel and ask. I was long overdue to pay my respects. Although, my father seemed more buried in my heart than in some cemetery plot.

Jeremy came into the living room and sat beside me. He looked out the window at the winter morning, at the garden that lay dormant, the rose bushes cut back, leafless, stunted. I gazed at the alders across the street, their spindly bare arms outstretched to the heavens. They seemed to be yearning for spring.

"What a beautiful day," he said, stroking my hair. "A new year. Full of promise."

He looked down at my belly and smiled at the life growing inside me. I felt strangely sad and joyous at the same time. And although I felt heavy with my pregnancy, heavy with anticipation and, admittedly, a little fear and worry over what the future held, something lifted off my heart. Some burden, a reprieve of sorts.

For years I had carried around my own poisonous guilt—for my failings as a dutiful daughter, my inability to make my mother happy, my lack as a wife. Even guilt over my miscarriages, as if I had done something wrong, so that I didn't deserve to have children. And now, after having found my father, Nathan Sitteroff, these self-recriminations were dissolving. I felt light, as if **flying**.

> I looked at Jeremy, **the only man I had ever loved, oh so loved**, and my heart soared like a helium-filled balloon escaping into the sky. I thought of **the man in the restaurant**—the man who had spent the better part of his life looking for answers. **Looking for truth**.
>
> **I'm free**, he said.
>
> I mouthed the words along with him.

That's how my book ends. The book begins with the conundrum of the man in the restaurant saying he is free, a man who is symbolic of Lisa and this journey of her life that has finally brought her to a place where she, too, feels free. The line about the only man she's ever loved "oh so loved" is an exact quote from the end of chapter one. Themes of freedom and a search for truth are at the heart of this story, so I wanted to be sure to bring them center stage at the very end.

When you can pull bits like this from your opening scene that are thematic to your story, they bring the novel around full circle and give the reader a sense of completion. As T. S. Eliot said: "In my end is my beginning." Strive to incorporate that thought as you create your ending.

One thing to note: my protagonist Lisa started off with one visible goal—to uncover the mystery surrounding her father's death, but in the end, she arrived at a completely unexpected place. The answer to her plot MDQ ("Will I save my brother by uncovering the truth of my father's death?") was no. But the answer to her spiritual MDQ ("Will this journey somehow bring peace and healing to my life, despite the risk?") was a resounding yes. You may decide your character won't reach her goal at all, though if she doesn't, there must be something invaluable she learns through the effort and makes the journey (and the ending of your novel) inevitable but not predictable.

Think about . . . pulling out those favorite novels on your shelves or skim through your e-reader to the last scene written of the novel you've just read. See how well the author accomplished all the things mentioned above. And take some notes as to what they did that was really well done.

If you're planning out an ending to your book, or feel maybe the one you have might not be quite right, think about your themes, motifs, and the heart of the story. Write a list of five possible scenarios for your ending that puts your character in a place and state of mind to be able to process what she's learned. Show how she now looks at the world, herself, her family, her life. What has become important to her now, at this moment, that wasn't before? What does she see as a powerful truth that she never saw before? Now that she's arrived at her visible goal, she's learned something significant, and if you can get that visually across, you're likely to have a powerful (but not necessarily explosive) ending to your book that will stick with your readers for a very long time.

If your novel is done, think about a motif or line from the first chapter that speaks to your theme (or put one in) and see how you can work it into your ending. Distill your ending down to just a few paragraphs and have your protagonist reflect on how she's now looking at the world with new sight, after what she's gone through. Take out every unnecessary word, any distracting description, that is not locking in on that moment.

## Chapter 29: The Universality Is in the Details

*"There's a universality in the story and it speaks to everyone."*
~actress Jacqueline Russell

I want to wrap up this book on the topic of universality since we want our novel's theme to have universal appeal—meaning a whole bunch of people all over the world should be able to relate to it at perhaps any time in history. But while we're thinking in broad, all-encompassing ideas, I want to make a distinction here.

Don't make the mistake in thinking that in order to appeal to a wide audience with a universal appeal we have to write in very general terms and details. You may think that the more *un*specific you can get with your locale, setting, time period, problems presented, the more universal the novel will be. You may think if your character can have a general problem—say a bad temper or he's a Scrooge—a lot of people will identify with him . . . so you decide to not be too specific and take the risk of making your novel's world so small that no one will relate.

### General Is Not Universal

Some authors have their characters in some unnamed place and time, engaging in activity and dialog in a way that philosophizes and narrates but is hard to picture. They think if they set their book in a certain time that in a decade or two it will read dated and won't endure as a classic.

What we learn by examining powerful novels that have stood the test of time is that they are exactly the opposite. They zoom in on a tiny moment in time in a very specific place. Sometimes that moment may just cover a few weeks and that place only one house on a block in a small town in the middle of nowhere. How about *To Kill a Mockingbird*? Of course, some books have a much wider landscape and could be epic novels, like those of James Michener. He actually felt brash enough to start one of his novels with the creation of the planet as the start of his story (can you name that novel?). But if you've read any of his books, you will know he's the king of detail.

I'm a big fan of Gabriel Garcia Marquez's books. Something he said in an interview really stuck with me decades ago and influenced my novel writing all the way through. Remembering what he said about detail inspired me to write this chapter, so I'm going to put a little excerpt of this interview with him from the Paris Review 1981 (which I happily found doing a Google search).

> **INTERVIEWER:** There also seems to be a journalistic quality to [your] technique or tone. You describe seemingly fantastic events in such minute detail that it gives them their own reality. Is this something you have picked up from journalism?
>
> **GARCÍA MÁRQUEZ:** That's a journalistic trick which you can also apply to literature. For example, if you say that there are elephants flying in the sky, people are not going to believe you. But if you say that there are four hundred and twenty-five elephants flying in the sky, people will probably believe you. *One Hundred Years of Solitude* is full of that sort of thing. That's exactly the technique my grandmother used. I remember particularly the story about the character who is surrounded by yellow butterflies. When I was very small there was an electrician who came to the house. I became very curious because he carried a belt with which he used to suspend himself from the electrical posts. My grandmother used to say that every time this man came around, he would leave the house full of butterflies.

> But when I was writing this, I discovered that if I didn't say the butterflies were yellow, people would not believe it. When I was writing the episode of Remedios the Beauty going to heaven, it took me a long time to make it credible. One day I went out to the garden and saw a woman who used to come to the house to do the wash and she was putting out the sheets to dry and there was a lot of wind. She was arguing with the wind not to blow the sheets away. I discovered that if I used the sheets for Remedios the Beauty, she would ascend. That's how I did it, to make it credible. The problem for every writer is credibility. Anybody can write anything so long as it's believed.

## Even One Little Adjective Can Do the Trick

This point about fine detail making a passage believable is such a great message for writers. Instead of shying away from being very specific in our scenes in order to achieve a universal appeal, think about making your small details very specific, the way a journalist would do if reporting an event they witness. You are like a reporter detailing events for your readers, so if you use detail like this, it adds believability. And believability is the key to universality.

> Think about . . . thinking like a journalist as you write or rework a scene. Everywhere you have general descriptions of things, come up with very specific details. Don't overload with details. Note that Marquez only needed to add the word **yellow** to make the appearance of butterflies seem real. A few specific details can be powerful, and they add clear imagery in your readers' heads, which is what you want.

## Chapter 30: The Secret to a Stress-free Novel Journey

*"It is good to have an end to journey toward, but it is the journey that matters in the end."*

~Ursula K. Le Guin

I saved this last bit for the end of the book, for either you've made it this far and are willing to listen to my spiel, or else you've given up and, in that case, you won't have to read this. But I'm going to stand on my soapbox and talk a little about the need to do some advance preparatory work.

I already mentioned this at the start of the book—and you've seen by all the topics we've covered—how there truly is a lot of thinking and figuring out that must be done before you dive into writing that novel. I know some of you will disagree with me, and as I said before, you have every right to do so. Write your own way. No one is holding a gun to your head. But I am hoping you will at least hear me out and give my advice a try.

At the risk of sounding repetitive (because I am being repetitive), you have a *choice*. You are not stuck in "pantser land." You really can learn how to plan out your novel before you start writing—and I truly believe if you do, you will find it a much more joyful experience. So here it is.

I'm going to paint a little analogy for you here about taking a trip—for writing your novel is a journey of sorts. And we have all probably had smooth-running trips as well as disastrous ones we'd rather forget (and wished we hadn't gone on).

## A Trip with Some Objectives in Mind

If you're like me, you like to have a sense of security in knowing the trip will be a good one, and that means planning in advance. Let's say you live in the US and you've never gone to Europe. You have three weeks, and you want to see about ten cities and visit two dozen major landmarks. So you go online, get brochures and maps, read reviews—do some research. Then you start working out an itinerary. Maybe you don't want to be so specific that you leave no room for spontaneity along the way. But you don't want to just hop on a plane to Frankfurt and wing it without even having booked your first night in a hotel. Of course, if you're out there looking for any kind of adventure and part of the thrill is seeing where you end up and wanting to be surprised (or mugged), that's a different kind of trip and doesn't apply here. I'm talking about a trip where you actually have some objectives in mind, some specific sights you really want to see and experience, and you don't want to waste a lot of time (or money) traveling needlessly on planes and trains in a haphazard fashion. You know that if you plan carefully, you'll pack in a lot of sights and go from one city to the next in an orderly manner.

## Don't End up Sleeping on a Bench in a Subway

By now you should know where I'm going with this. If you don't want to hear the lecture, skip to the last page. But I hope you'll hear me out (you can make faces at me since I can't see you). Writers who dive into a project as huge and challenging as writing a novel without planning much ahead of time are taking many risks. They may go off on a journey that wastes their time and resources (emotional ones primarily) and doesn't bring them a lot of joy. They may experience a large amount of stress by not having things planned ahead, similar to having to sleep sitting on a bench in some subway because all the hotels in town are booked for a large event that they were unaware of because they didn't do their research.

A trip taken without enough advanced preparation foments too much undue stress—stress that could have been avoided if some time had been taken to plan it out better. Travelers embarking on such an unclear journey face one unexpected problem after another as they try to get to where they wanted to go. The journey becomes a big hassle and not a whole lot of fun. I don't want to be stressed out when I'm taking my coveted vacation. I aim to relax and have fun. What about you?

## Planning Does Leave Room for Spontaneity

If you want to write a novel that is going to "visit" certain "places" and eventually gets to a final destination, you're going to have more success and less stress if you take some time (days, weeks) to plan it out in advance. I don't like to use the word *plot* because it implies putting a novel together is all about plot, and it's not. You can use the word if you like; I'm not stopping you.

I would like you to imagine for a moment that this journey you want to take, which you hope will be memorable and wonderful—a journey of the heart—is like a well-planned trip. If you work out the major details, such as itinerary and flights and sights you want to see, you can still leave plenty of room for variation and exploration.

When my husband and I went to London a few years ago for three weeks, we had a lot of places we wanted to see around the country. But we wanted to be spontaneous too, so we booked a flat in London for the first week, to get us there. We knew a week would give us time to see all the museums and sights on our list. Once we were there, we kicked around ideas of where to go next, but before the week was out, we had the next week sketched in. We decided to head over to Bath (a city I love but one Lee had never been to) for a few days. Once there, we explored the surrounding region, then booked a room in an inn up in York and spent most of a week there. We had hoped to get to many other places, but we found there wasn't enough time to thoroughly enjoy our trip if we just whizzed through each town without spending some time in each place. We decided those other destinations would have to be visited during another trip to England. (And yes, we took our little garden gnome with us so we could give him a vacation too and take photos of him—just like in *Amélie*.)

## Planning Keeps You (Mostly) on Course

Sometimes when we write a novel—whether we're winging it off the top of our heads or following an outline—we tend to get distracted and veer off in another direction. Our characters like to take over and insist on doing things we didn't plan. Sometimes that works great—it's often your intuition and creativity leading you in a better direction than the one you first had. Much like arriving in a town you thought you'd stay in for days, but when you take a side trip you find this new town an even better place to visit, so you change your reservations and head out.

But when you have a solid framework for your novel, knowing your objectives, goals, themes, plot and character arcs (don't get me started again on the *arc* thing), you won't veer far off course. In fact, if you do start wandering down a dark alley, you'll stop and go back because you know right away it's not fitting in with the kind of trip you had in mind. On the other hand, if you're just writing "by the seat of your pants," and you veer off in some odd direction (which will happen *most* of the time you're writing because you really have *no idea* where you want to go or what you want to do at all on this trip other than "have fun" or "experience life" or something vague like that), your trip is going to be a real mess and a disappointment (to you and everyone else you've dragged along with you) .

Enough said? I don't want to be so brash as to say that a lot of writers don't plan their books ahead because they're lazy or they're afraid planning will take away from the joy of being spontaneously creative. I can't speak to the first part of that statement; only you know why you won't take the time to plan your novel in advance. But I can speak to the second part, as I hope I've conveyed above. You *don't* squelch your creativity by constructing a detailed framework in which to tell your story. You actually set up a place for your creativity to explode in greatness. A piano has only eighty-eight keys—that's the framework in which a composer has to create a piano piece. And yet untold numbers of amazing musical compositions have been written within that framework.

## Winging It with a Prayer

I will simply summarize by saying I really don't believe you can write a great novel by winging it. I know I probably offended a bunch of you seat-of-the-pants writers out there, but I have to say this. Maybe you have a gift and can throw things out from the top of your head and they'll land in perfect positioning in your novel. No? The answer I usually get from "pantsers" is that they have to spend months rewriting, revising, reworking again and again until some beauty comes from the ashes.

I mentioned this in the beginning of this book—how many authors will throw out draft after draft until they figure out their story. A lot of famous authors like Stephen King will swear that all first drafts are terrible. King would say this, because he's not a plotter. But who I am to argue with any method Stephen King touts? And it's safe to assume he's written enough novels that he has basic structure ingrained in his brain and does much of that planning automatically.

Still, I am going to go against the grain here and beg to differ and offer you another way. And really, it's fine if you disagree with me. I would just like to encourage you to consider it.

The main reason I advocate serious planning before writing a novel is for efficiency of time. Frankly, I don't have months to waste rewriting and rewriting. I have way too many things to do in my life, and I usually have two novels I want to write a year (while working full-time as a copyeditor and writing coach), so I don't have time to mess around with going from really raw material to polish. I truly believe you can write a really good first draft of your entire novel that will only require a tiny bit of reworking or polishing when done.

I'm a bit like Dean Koontz, who revises and edits as he goes along so that when he finishes his last chapter, he's pretty much done. I'm that way with all my novels. I almost never rewrite, delete or add a scene, or do much other than copyedit and proofread. On occasion my test readers will point out some dufus plot hole I missed or note a passage that needs work and I'll attend to those. But when I'm done writing my novel in two, three, four months, and I write "the end," I pretty much mean "the end." I'm done.

## I'm No One Special

You may think I'm unusual and you could never do that. But I disagree. I think a lot of writers shy away from putting in the work needed before starting a novel. But again, I'm looking at the big picture—the amount of time that you're going to put into your novel from start to polished finish. So think about it—you can spend a few weeks really plotting out your novel, developing rich characters, honing your themes, motifs, and heart of the story before you jump in and write. Or you can spend *many months* agonizing over numerous rewrites in a cloud of confusion.

Personally, I'd rather work out all the rough spots and challenging aspects *first* so they don't get in the way. So I can enjoy writing and know the story is working already as I put the words down. Folks, I just *don't* have time to waste, nor do I want to subject myself to that kind of frustrating, disappointing, depressing method of writing. I am sure I would just quit writing with that kind of grief. I'm not a masochist, although I suspect some writers are. I would think most writers would feel the same way I do, though. It's no fun winging it with a prayer that your book might actually hold together when you're done.

## Don't Knock It if You Haven't Tried It

If your time is valuable and you'd like to save a few months of your time for other things, like being with your family (remember them?), maybe you'll reconsider and change your attitude about planning your book in advance. I read how Toni Morrison says that by the time she sits at her computer to write, she's already done all the hard work—thinking, musing, figuring out the story she wants to tell. Don't knock it until you've tried it. There are many other reasons for planning in advance, aside from the time component, such as you really do end up with a tighter, better written book (okay, that's my opinion, for what it's worth), but *planning shows.* It does. And it just makes your writing life a whole lot easier. Trust me—you are not squelching your creativity or denying yourself a measure of spontaneity by planning in advance

Think about . . . the novel you're just getting started on. Don't rush to jump in and start writing. Spend some time thinking about the big elements you want in your book. Spend some days writing about your characters, even freewriting in their voice to let them speak to you. Try taking a walk, talking out loud or mulling over the story and why you're writing it, what you want to say, and how you want to say it. (A good tip is to keep a tiny notebook and pen in your pocket, or use the notes app or voice memo program, as I do, on my iPhone, so as I get ideas, I can jot them down or record them when driving or walking.) Resist the urge to write from the top of your head, and let those ideas first simmer and boil down into something concise and clear. You may find you like this!

# Epilogue: Looking Back over the Journey to the Heart

*"The idea is to write so that people hear it, and it slides through the brain and goes straight to the heart."*

~Maya Angelou

We've taken a long journey from the entrance to the mine to the heart of your story, where the mother lode of gold is hidden. The objective? To create an unforgettable, great novel that speaks to the heart of the reader—hopefully transcending the restrictions of time and place. By aiming for the heart with universal themes, rich characters, and carefully constructed scenes, you might just produce a novel that will live in the hearts of readers for generations—a novel we might call timeless.

When we think of Shakespeare's plays, written hundreds of years ago, so widely loved and praised, what are the elements that resonate with us? Wouldn't you say they are his universal themes that apply to everyone in every time period? What about his engaging, complex, believable characters who are rich with history, full of needs and dreams, believing lies they've been told? We wouldn't leave out his biting humor or witty turn of a phrase, and not everyone is a master wordsmith. But literary works that have stood the test of time can teach us much about getting to the heart of our story.

## Read, Read, Read

One bit of great advice I've heard throughout my years as a writer is the need to read—widely and deeply. Read the classics, the best of various genres, books that are still being reprinted after a hundred years. Stretch yourself by reading some books in genres you wouldn't think to read. Maybe you've never read a Western or a Jane Austen novel. I'm not saying you have to love every book that has sold over a million copies at some point in time. But with your eyes trained now to know how to reach the heart of a story, you can read these novels with a keen awareness, studying how the scenes are built, how the characters are portrayed and how they interact with their world, how the setting is painted. You can tear apart the first scene, see how many elements in that scene match up with the First-Page Checklist. You can look at the tone and the voice of the characters, see what motifs are brought out, and how the quality of time is handled.

So much can be learned by studying the craft of great writers. That's not to say you want to copy what they do so precisely that you are solely derivative or plagiarizing. However, if you take the time and deconstruct or break down great novels, you can learn much from those who have mined to the heart of their stories with great success.

Sometimes we writers feel like our well of creativity has run dry. The best way I know to fill it back up again is to read great novels, plays, poetry, and short stories. When I read a terrific passage in a novel, I feel uplifted and energized. As I mentioned in the first chapter, books that are beautifully written, that speak to our hearts, are gems in a mine full of dull rocks. A great book feeds our soul and nourishes our spirit in a way nothing else can.

And now that you know the way to the heart of your story, my hope is that you will create gems of your own—novels that will stand the test of time by speaking to the heart. As William Wordsworth encouraged: "Fill your paper with the breathings of your heart."

Shore up that entrance to your mine with careful planning, then be the light showing the way through the dark, winding tunnel to the mother lode. And don't forget to enjoy the journey—with all its bumps and pitfalls. Remember, starting is better than finishing. But I will now add this: Finishing can be just as great at starting—if the end of your story ends at the heart.

## About the Author

C. S. Lakin is a multipublished novelist and writing coach who loves to help writers find joy and success in their novel-writing journey. She works full-time as a copyeditor (fiction and nonfiction) and critiques about two hundred manuscripts a year. She teaches writing workshops around the country and gives instruction on her award-winning blog Live Write Thrive (www.livewritethrive.com).

Her grammar book—*Say What? The Fiction Writer's Handy Guide to Grammar, Punctuation, and Word Usage*—is designed to help writers get a painless grasp on grammar. You can buy it in print or as an ebook.

Connect with her on Twitter and Facebook.

Lakin lives in a small town south of San Francisco, CA, with her husband Lee, a gigantic lab named Coaltrane, and three persnickety cats. She loves to hike and backpack, cook, and spend time with her two daughters and grandson.

## Want to become the best novelist you can be?

The Writer's Toolbox series will give you all the tools you need to write terrific, well-structured stories that will stand the test of time and scrutiny.

If you benefited from Writing the Heart of Your Story, be sure to get Shoot Your Novel—an essential writing craft guide that will teach you the art of "show don't tell" using time-tested cinematic technique. In this era of visual media, readers want more than ever to "see" stories unfold before their eyes. By utilizing film technique and adapting the various camera shots into your fiction, your writing will undergo a stunning transformation from "telling" to "showing."

## Here's a sneak peek at *Shoot Your Novel*, releasing fall, 2014:

# Shoot Your Novel
## Cinematic Techniques to Supercharge Your Writing

## INTRODUCTION
## POINT AND SHOOT

So, a man walks into a bar, accompanied by a large piece of asphalt. He goes up to the bartender and says, "I'll have a whiskey." He nods at his friend and adds, "Oh, and one for the road."

If I told this joke to you and a group of your friends, I'm not sure you'd laugh as much as I'd hope, but one thing I am sure of—you would each have pictured this playing out in your head, and each would have seen a completely different "movie." Maybe you pictured this taking place in a Western saloon, with the man dressed in cowboy boots and wearing a Stetson hat. He probably had a Texan drawl, and maybe was chewing tobacco as he spoke. Maybe one of your friends imagined a Yuppie high-end urban bar, with soft leather upholstery and smelling of expensive Cuban cigar smoke.

However you envisioned this briefly described scene, no doubt your friends "saw" something wholly different in their minds. Here's the point: if you had watched this in a movie on the big screen, you and your friends would have seen the exact same things. You wouldn't be arguing later whether the piece of asphalt was black or gray or the man was wearing that hat or not. The film itself provided all the details for you, leaving little to your imagination.

### Tell It Like You See It

With fiction, though, writers are presented with an entirely different situation. The reader reading your novel will only see the specifics if you detail them. And even if you do, it's likely she will still envision many of the scene elements different from what you hoped to convey.

That's not necessarily a bad thing. In fact, leaving out details and allowing the reader to "fill in the blanks" is part of the reader-writer relationship. In a way, a novel becomes much more personal than a movie, a little bit of a "choose your own adventure" quality. Many love novels just for that ability to "put themselves" into the story, whether it be by relating to a protagonist, seeing people we know in the characters presented, or feeling like we are going through the trials and perils presented by the plot.

The challenge and beauty of the artistic palette a writer uses raises numerous questions:

- How much or how little detail do I (or should I) put in my novel in order to help the reader see the story the way I see it? And how much should I leave to the reader's imagination?

- How can I best write each scene so that I "show" the reader what I want him to see?

- How can I write scenes that will give the emotional impact equivalent to what can be conveyed through a film?

The joke I told was short and didn't give much detail. It had no power or punch, no strong feel of action or movement. I doubt you will remember it a month from now. Other than the man walking and talking and nodding, the "scene" was stagnant, with little to stir the imagination or evoke emotion. Maybe your own writing feels this way to you—often—and you don't know what to do to make it better. Maybe you've read a dozen books on the writing craft and have attended countless workshops at writers' conferences and you still can't seem to "get" how to write powerful, evocative scenes that move your readers. Well, if you sometimes feel like strangling, stabbing, or decapitating your novel because of flat, boring, lackluster scenes, you can *shoot* your novel instead!

## Show, Don't Tell—But How?

Sol Stein, in his book *Stein on Writing*, says, "Twentieth-century readers, transformed by film and TV, are used to *seeing* stories. The reading experience for a twentieth-century reader is increasingly visual. The story is happening in front of his eyes." This is even more true in the twenty-first century. As literary agent and author Donald Maass says in *Writing 21st Century Fiction*: "Make characters do something that readers can visualize."

We've heard it countless times: show, don't tell. Sounds simple, right? Wrong. There are a myriad of choices a writer has to make in order to "show" and not "tell" a scene. Writers are often told they need to show, which in essence means to create visual scenes the reader can "watch" unfold as they read.

But telling a writer to "show" is vague. Just how do you show? How do you transfer the clearly enacted scene playing in your mind to the page in a way that not only gets the reader to see just what you want her to see but also comes across with the emotional impact you intend?

## The Shotgun Method

Writers know that if they say "Jane was terrified," that only *tells* the reader what Jane is feeling; it doesn't *show* her terrified. So they go on to construct a scene that shows Jane in action and *reacting* to the thing that inspires fear in her. And somehow in doing so writers hope they will make their reader afraid too. But that's often like using a shotgun approach. You aim at a target from a hundred yards away with a shotgun and hope a few buckshot pellets actually hit the bull's eye. Many writers think if they just "point and shoot" they will hit their target every time. But then, when they get lackluster reviews, or dozens of agent or publisher rejections, they can't figure out what they did wrong, or failed to do. Why is this? Is there some "secret formula" to writing visually impacting scenes every time?

No, not secret. In fact, the method is staring writers in the face; we have all been raised watching thousands of movies and television shows. The style, technique, and methods used in film and TV are so familiar to us, we process them comfortably and even subconsciously. We now expect these elements to appear in the novels we read, to some degree—if not consciously then subconsciously.

Filmmaker Gustav Mercado, in his book *The Filmmaker's Eye*, makes this very observation about movies, stating that cinematic tradition has become standardized in the way the rules of composition are applied to certain camera shots "which over time have linked key moments in a story with the use of particular shots." His "novel" approach, which he claims is new, is to examine the shot as "a deeper and discursive exploration into the fundamental elements of the visual language of cinema." If this has been proven true with camera technique, it stands to reason the same idea would transfer over into writing fiction. If novelists can learn how filmmakers utilize particular camera shots to achieve specific effects, create specific moods, and evoke specific emotions, they have a powerful tool at hand.

We know what makes a great, riveting scene in a movie, and what makes a boring one—at least viscerally. And though our tastes differ, certainly, for the most part we often agree when a scene "works" or doesn't. It either accomplishes what the writer or director has set out to do, or it flops.

So since we have all been (over)exposed to film and its visual way of storytelling, and its influence on society has altered the tastes of fiction readers, it's only logical to take a look at what makes a great movie. Note that we're not looking at plot or premise in this book, for that's an entirely different subject. Instead, we're going to deconstruct movie technique into bite-sized pieces.

Just as your novel comprises a string of scenes that flow together to tell your whole story, so too with movies and television shows. However, you, the novelist, lay out your scenes much differently from the way a screenwriter does. Whereas you might see each of your scenes as integrated, encapsulated moments of time, a movie director sees each scene as a compilation of a number of segments or pieces—a collection of camera shots that are subsequently edited and fit together to create that seamless "moment of time."

## Time to Put On a New Hat

So take off your writer hat for a minute and put on a director one—you know, that sun visor you see the director wear as he's looking through the camera eyepiece on the outdoor set of the big studio lot and as he thinks how he's going to shoot the next scene. Have you ever watched a behind-the-scenes look at how a movie is being filmed, or a TV series? I love watching and listening to Peter Jackson in his many videos detailing the filming of both *The Lord of the Rings* and *The Hobbit* feature films. Jackson does a wonderful job showing the kinds of decisions he has to make as he ponders the shooting of a scene in order to get across the impact, mood, details, and key moments he desires in the final cut.

Directors have to plan like this. They can't show up on the set each morning and look at the shooting schedule and just "wing it." A large sum of money is riding on the director doing his homework and knowing exactly what each scene must convey and show to the viewer. Directors decide just how a scene will be shown and what specifically will be focused on. Using the camera, a director can basically "force" viewers to see exactly what he wants them to see. And one goal in doing this is to evoke a particular emotional reaction from them.

## Writing Is Not All That Different from Directing

Writers can do the same. They may not be able to paint so specific a picture that every single reader will envision a novel exactly the same—and that's a good thing. In fact, that's what makes reading novels so . . . well, novel. Readers infuse their personalities, backgrounds, fears, and dreams into a book as they read. A character named Tiffany will conjure up a face for me different from the one you picture in your head. In this way, novels are an interactive experience—the reader's imagination interacting with the novelist's.

Yet, writers can also put on their director's hat—and well they should. Remember, readers nowadays want to read books that are more visual, as Stein remarked—scenes that are happening right before their eyes. But few writers are ever shown just how to do this effectively, and that's what this book is about. You don't have to guess anymore how to "show" a scene in a way that's "supercharged." By learning to use camera shots the way a director does, you too can take readers where you want them to go, make them see what you want them to see. Don't leave that up to the reader to decide. Be not just the writer but the director. Filmmaker Gustav Mercado makes a succinct point in his book: "You should not be subservient to the dictates of a technique but make the technique work for the specific needs of your story instead." What a great truth for both novelists and filmmakers.

So get out of your cozy office chair and follow me onto the set where all the great movies are filmed. Get out your writers' toolbox and be prepared to add a whole new layer of tools—camera shots. Once you learn what these are and how to use them in writing fiction, it's more than likely you will never write the same way again—or look at a scene the same way.

And I truly hope so. I hope once you grab these cinematic secrets and supercharge your novel, you will never take that shotgun out again and just "point and shoot." Instead, you will be the director looking at the scene from all angles and making deliberate decisions on which camera angles to use for the greatest impact.

# CHAPTER 1: IT'S ALL ABOUT THE ANGLE

Having spent my entire childhood at the feet of my screenwriter mother, I read more TV scripts than books while growing up, as there were piles of them around my mother's office, and I'd often curl up on the couch and read one after school. I also spent many hours on sound stages and on location watching many of her TV episodes being filmed. Okay, I will confess I liked to sit in Peggy Lipton's chair during the shooting of *Mod Squad*, and if we were outside I wore my mirror shades to be in sync with the dynamic threesome I admired (I rarely saw Clarence Williams III ever take his shades off—indoors or outdoors). I spent many hours wandering in and out of sound stages at Fox, MGM, and other studios where my mother, for a time, had an office. I'd sneak into *M.A.S.H* and watch the banter Alan Alda tossed around as he operated on a fake body in the surgery tent, or mosey on over to *Battlestar Gallactica.* I had fun going on location and even spent a week in San Francisco on the set with Rock Hudson (*MacMillan and Wife*), since my stepfather was the director of that episode, and got to watch some cool stunts involving cable cars (no, Rock didn't do his own stunts!).

I say all this to make the point that growing up in a home that centered around writing and directing for television greatly influenced the way I approach storytelling. Ever since I learned the alphabet, I wrote stories. I even pitched my first script idea at age twelve to the producer of *The Girl from U.N.C.L.E.* Do you remember that show? (Okay just so you know, Stephanie Powers starred in it, and Ian Fleming was the consultant on the show and suggested the idea, but it only ran twenty-nine episodes before being canceled for low ratings. Maybe if they had bought my idea and wrote that script, it wouldn't have failed. Hmm, I wonder . . .) I still have my very polite rejection letter—my first of many! It did help that my mother was a staff writer on the show and had "an in." However, they didn't buy my idea. But you can be sure of one thing—even at age twelve I presented my idea to the producer in a way he could easily visualize it as an episode. My young mind was already programmed to write cinematically.

So when I began writing novels decades later (although I promised my mother I would never be a writer, but that's another story), it was only natural for me to construct all my scenes visually, the way I might see them play out on film. In fact, I couldn't imagine writing any differently. I'm not surprised when I continually get comments from readers like, "I could so picture this book as a movie" or "this novel would make a great movie." I believe they say these things not so much because they think my books are brilliant but because I write *cinematically*. Every scene is structured either consciously or unconsciously with a series of camera shots, so the reader will see the scene play out the way *I* see it.

I'm very familiar with the camera shots used—and as I mentioned before, you really are too. If you've watched a few TV shows or seen a few movies, you're already familiar with what I'm going to share with you. What you don't yet know, possibly, is how to *transcribe* what you see on the screen to the words on your pages. So I'm going to deconstruct movie technique by examining the camera shots one by one, and showing examples in novels in which the writer has effectively used a particular camera angle (or multiple angles) to create a supercharged scene.

## Varieties of Camera Angles for Specific Effects

Screenplays are structured through the use of camera direction, which becomes all-important to telling the story. The choice of camera angles within a scene affects the mood, focus, and emphasis of the story being told, and directs the viewer to pay attention to particular elements unfolding. The right camera angle will give the best impact: you wouldn't film a huge explosion using a Close-up but rather a Long Shot encompassing the wide scope of action. Writers, too, should think about not just the character POV (point of view) of a scene but the camera angles. Don't leave it up to the reader to figure out what is important to notice. Put on your director's hat and think what shots will focus on what's important. By using these filming techniques to point your reader's attention where *you* want it to go, you will get the results you want.

## Don't Be Boring

Most authors use the same angle in every scene, and that can be boring. What do I mean by "the same angle"? I mean that if there was a camera filming what was taking place in the scene, it would be set up in one spot and never move. It would never zoom in, PAN, pull back, or follow anyone. Is that bad? Not necessarily. You may have a scene that is solely in a character's head—just her thinking. And maybe that's a powerful scene because of the character and plot points revealed. But would you enjoy reading a book in which most of the scenes were like that? Probably not. In fact, if you read a few pages of explanation and internal thinking and *nothing was happening* (read: no real-time playing out of a scene you can visualize), you just might throw the book down and go get a bowl of ice cream to soothe your battered soul.

## It's Just Not Happening

Haven't you read scenes where two people are sitting somewhere (and you've probably not been told where) and just talking? The dialog goes on for pages, and maybe some of it is interesting, but you can't picture where these people are, what the setting is like, what they look like. Or maybe you have more description than you want—of the restaurant and their clothes and hair and the noise and smells inside. But still—nothing *happens.*

I'm not talking about physical action. And this is an important distinction. There can be a lot happening in a scene without a character even twitching. There can be heavy subtext, innuendo, clues, suspicions—all kinds of tension and plot reveals going on. But still, the scene can feel flat and a bit boring because it feels like the camera filming all this is stuck in one spot across the room.

This is not to say every scene needs to have your "camera" zooming and panning and doing gymnastics to keep your reader's interest up. But once you see how you can bring in a variety of camera shots to your scenes—even the ones in which not much is happening—you will realize there are better ways to construct them to supercharge them.

Don't settle for okay or boring or so-so. Think *big impact.* That's what great directors do. And big impact doesn't apply to just explosive scenes with high action. You can have a huge-impact small moment. A tiny element in your story can be key—the gripping pivot upon which your entire plot hinges—and by using the right camera shots, you can play up that subtle bit and blow it up to the size it should be. High-impact moments, regardless of how subtle, should "fill the entire screen." And I'll show you how it can be done.

## The Art of Film Editing

Have you ever watched old black-and-white movies? I'm thinking in particular of those great Fred Astaire musicals full of amazing dance routines. Sometime, go watch a few and pay attention to the camera shot. Back in the day, film editing was kept to a minimum. It was expensive, tedious work. Film editors had to literally cut and splice pieces of film together, which was tricky to do seamlessly. Because of this, most of those great dance numbers are one long shot from one camera, without interruptions, without slicing and dicing. Not like what's done today. It makes me wonder how many takes Fred and Ginger had to do to get one good keeper shot. I get tired just thinking about all those fast, nifty steps.

Today editing is a highly praised art form, and with the current tech is much easier and versatile. A film editor must creatively work with the layers of images, story, dialogue, music, pacing, as well as the actors' performances to effectively "re-imagine" and even rewrite the film to craft a cohesive whole. Editors usually play a dynamic role in the making of a film. Walter Murch once said, "Film editing is now something almost everyone can do at a simple level and enjoy it, but to take it to a higher level requires the same dedication and persistence that any art form does."

The editing in film often goes unnoticed. However, if one does not notice the editing, then it is doing its job. The editor works on the subconscious of the viewer, and if you think about it, writers do the same when they write a novel. Editors are awarded Academy Awards, and maybe you've wondered why, but I don't.

Now, you may think it really odd, but knowing my background, you should understand when I say one of the things I pay the most attention to when I watch a movie (and comment on to my husband—to which he can attest!) is the editing. I feel the editing is what makes the movie. A terrifically edited movie scores more points in my book than a well-written one. I am enthralled when I watch a beautifully edited movie, when all the cuts of the various camera shots are pieced together like a symphony.

One movie that comes to mind is *Inception*. There are sequences in that movie that are edited to show reality unfolding on three different dream levels all at the same time. It is masterfully done. If you've watched the opening scene of *Saving Private Ryan* and you felt like your heart was being ripped out, much of that was due to the brilliant, powerful editing. Although I could barely view the painful images on the screen (and I'm glad I saw it on my small TV and not in a theater), I can't forget specific camera angles used, such as the shot taken from the seaward side of the landing craft looking toward the beach as the Allied soldiers try to disembark and are mowed down with machine-gun fire, many while still in the boat, the water turning red as bodies keep falling.

In contrast, a movie with boring editing will tend to show boring scenes that feel flat or choppy or lacking spark.

## Yes, Another Hat

If you haven't figured out by now where I'm going with this, I hope you won't be surprised to have me tell you that, yes, you also need to wear that editor's hat. I don't mean the "book" kind of editor, like me, but the movie kind I mentioned above—the person who takes the film of all the raw footage of the shot scenes and pieces it together in not just the right order but in a specific sequence.

Think about it. Each scene in a movie or TV show is not just shot from one angle; it's shot from many. There are close shots in which you see one character's face and the back of another's head. There are stationary shots taken from different angles, as well as numerous moving shots taken from different angles. You may have an aerial shot, some long shots, some tilted ones, some tracking shots done with the camera moving along on a dolly. The director will make clear which shots he wants. He then, along with various producers and others, will work with the film editor to choose which shots to use in a scene, and like a jigsaw puzzle will (hopefully) seamlessly put it together so it flows without lagging, as well as provides just the right tension and pacing needed.

It's not easy. And novelists have to do exactly the same thing. They have to not only "shoot" their scenes, they have to choose the camera angles, and then piece it all together in a way that fits their genre and story, and keeps the pacing going at the speed needed to engage the reader. A novel set in Victorian England showing the characters having tea and discussing suitable marriage prospects (not my cup of tea) should have different camera shots and entirely different editing than a suspense thriller in which the protagonist has to save the world before the ticking bomb explodes.

## CUT TO: An Important Point

I want to say "cut" here to emphasize something I need to talk about and will reiterate throughout this book, and that's the importance of being aware of the "high moment" of each of your scenes. This is what good directors know. Before they shoot that scene on their shooting schedule for the day, they are thinking about that instant (whether it will last a few seconds or even a minute) the scene is building to.

Without going into a treatise about scene construction (which I do in my book *Writing the Heart of Your Story*), suffice it to say each scene must have a point to it or it shouldn't be in your novel. If you have scenes with no "point," you need to either give them a point or throw them out. Too many writers write too many scenes with no point to them. Filmmaker Gustav Mercado says to create powerful impact, the technical elements, compositional choices, and narrative content should all work in context to create *meaning*. Without meaning, what is the point of telling your story?

Ever seen a movie that left you scratching your head? A movie with scenes that had no point to them, and for the life of you, you couldn't figure out why they were in the movie at all? Same thing. Someone should have cut those scenes out or rewritten them, you think. Maybe you've said that about scenes you've read in some novels too. Hopefully no one has said that about your novels, but if they have, you can fix that. How? By making sure you have a high moment you are building to.

A high moment doesn't have to be a huge moment. Remember, what's significant to a reader is what impacts the character. Just a single word can pack a punch in a scene, and often does. A beautifully delivered line of dialog can be more explosive than blowing up the Statue of Liberty. Great movie directors know this too. As actress Rosalind Russell said, what makes a great movie is "moments." And in order to write supercharged scenes that utilize specific camera shots, you have to know what moment you are building to. Just keep that in mind.

## A String of Shots Equals a Scene

Movies are made up of a string of shot sequences—don't confuse these with whole scenes. In creating a shot sequence, the aim of using a camera is to imitate the way the human mind uses the eyes. Our minds will not let our eyes stay fixed on any one subject for more than four or five seconds. Our eyes are constantly moving and focusing on different subjects.

For example, you may be walking down the street and you come across two of your friends having a small picnic at one of the tables in the city park at the corner. Your mind will probably direct your eyes into the following views of the couple:

- First, you would have a Wide-Angle or Long Shot of the entire scene.

- As you walk toward the couple, you will look at one person, and then the other.

- As you come closer, you might shift your focus and look at what is on the table.

- Your next glance will probably be at the first person who speaks to you.

- As the conversation continues, your eyes will shift from person to person, from person to table, from an action of one person to that person's face etc., etc. The combinations could be endless.

This type of realistic behavior is what you want to capture in your fiction writing, and the way to do it is by utilizing various camera angles, the difference being that you have a *specific intention* in doing so. Rather than show a random encounter with boring dialog and nothing all that interesting happening in the scene—which is what real life often is like—you have an objective in playing this scene out, that high point you are leading to, a moment of revelation or plot twist that is going to deliver with a punch when you reach it. And so every camera angle is used deliberately to give the most punch when needed.

Television producers follow a basic rule that no shot should last more than thirty seconds, and no scene should last longer than three minutes. This is the 30-3 Rule. This is the basic idea of how shot sequences are made. You take one long scene and break it down into a variety of short shots.

How does this translate to fiction? A scene can take much longer than three minutes to read, and sometimes it may cover a number of moments in time, some even separated by days and weeks. But if you break down your scenes and look at the segments that take place, you will find a natural rhythm that feels just right. Scenes should be mini novels, with a beginning, middle, and end. It doesn't work to place strict rules on scenes, for they should be as long as they need to be—whatever it takes to effectively reveal the bit of storyline intended while keeping the pacing and tension taut. However, I believe if you lay out your scenes intentionally with a series of camera shots, leaving out excessive narration and backstory, your scenes will "move" like a movie and will feel like concise, succinct movie scenes.

## Two Types of Camera Shots

Essentially, there are two types of camera shots—stationary and moving. I've never seen them classified this way, so I use these terms I came up with. Or you could think of them as static and dynamic, or still and kinetic. Use whatever terms work for you. But basically we're talking about filming a moment in which the camera is either moving or not moving. Simple.

You decide which types of camera shots you will use based on your high moment. If the high point of your scene involves showing an expression on someone's face, an object (like a ring), a small detail not before noticed, then the key camera shot will be a Close-up (CU), which might also be called a Close Shot, or it might be Angle On. If the high moment will be a sudden massive explosion due to an unnoticed gas leak, the key moment will require a Pull Back (PB) and/or a Long Shot (LS). By knowing the key moment and how your plot builds to it, you can plan the camera angles to best enhance the visual experience and evoke the strongest emotional reaction from your reader.

Of course, your scenes have more to them than just the high moment, and for that reason, you will need to use a number of camera angles for each scene, for the most part. But I bring up the need to first identify your high moment and determine what shot is needed *then*, for that's the moment of greatest impact and needs the most emphasis. Once you know how you will show that moment, you can work backward and forward, figuring out the rest of the shots. This is just my method. I have no idea if movie directors think this way or plan each scene out in any particular fashion. Maybe some work chronologically, deciding on the first shot and going from there. But I believe if you use this method, it will best serve you and the needs of your plot.

So as we go through these stationary and moving camera shots, think about when you might want to keep the "camera still" and when you want to move it from one place to another. As you will see, there's a specific purpose to each shot.

Made in the USA
Middletown, DE
02 August 2016